John Ford on location
during the prewar years

John Ford and the
American West

John Ford and the American West

Peter Cowie

HARRY N. ABRAMS, INC. PUBLISHERS

For my father, who first took me to Westerns

Project Manager: Harriet Whelchel
Editor: Richard Slovak
Designer: Miko McGinty
Production Manager: Maria Pia Gramaglia

LIBRARY OF CONGRESS CATALOGING-IN-PUBLICATION DATA

Cowie, Peter.
  John Ford and the American West / Peter Cowie.
     p. cm.
  Filmography: p.
  Includes bibliographical references and index.
  ISBN 0–8109–4976–8 (hardcover)
  1. Ford, John, 1894–1973—Criticism and interpretation.
I. Title.

  PN1998.3.F65C68 2004
  791.4302'33'092—dc22

                              2004013253

Published in 2004 by Harry N. Abrams,
Incorporated, New York

Printed and bound in Singapore

10 9 8 7 6 5 4 3 2 1

Harry N. Abrams, Inc.
100 Fifth Avenue
New York, N.Y. 10011
www.abramsbooks.com

Abrams is a subsidiary of

LA MARTINIÈRE

Contents

INTRODUCTION

There have been several good books on the life and work of John Ford. His prodigious career—some 220 films (including documentaries and short subjects) directed or produced over a span of fifty-three years—ranged over many genres and many different phases of Hollywood history.

The concept of family predominates not just in Ford's Westerns but also in *The Grapes of Wrath,* with Jane Darwell (left), Charley Grapewin (right), and Henry Fonda (seated, center).

When addressing the Screen Directors Guild in 1950, Ford introduced himself with almost Wellesian modesty: "My name's John Ford. I make Westerns." I would never assert that Ford's only claim to classic status lies in his Westerns, but I do believe that he was most at ease when filming in the great outdoors, and that in such films he could create—perhaps "craft" is a better term—a vision of his country's past that accorded with his Irish-American sentiments. And, as this book seeks to show, Ford's Westerns flowed from a vibrant tradition in the visual arts— a tradition rooted in the aspirations of Manifest Destiny, the belief that propelled American society westward during the nineteenth century.

To illustrate the links between Ford's vision and that of the nineteenth-century painters he admired so much, I have devoted most of this book to the major Westerns, while including other Ford films that impinge on that vision, such as *Young Mr. Lincoln* and *The Horse Soldiers*. His private life and the triumphs and vagaries of his long career, however, have already been well covered in biographies galore. Suffice it to say that John Ford was born John Martin Feeney, the tenth child of Irish immigrants living in Cape Elizabeth, Maine, in 1894 (not Sean Aloysius O'Feeney in 1895, as many sources have it). He grew up proud of his Irish ancestry, and he would refer to it directly in such films as *The Informer* and *The Quiet Man*, as well as indirectly in films like *How Green Was My Valley* and *The Grapes of Wrath*, which though not set in Ireland reflect the poverty and family loyalties Ford associated with the land of his forebears. Ford told Peter Bogdanovich that the Okie migration from Oklahoma to California in *The Grapes of Wrath* (1940) "appealed to me—being about simple people—and the story was similar to the Famine in Ireland, when they threw the people off the land and left them wandering on the roads to starve. That may have something to do with it—part of my Irish tradition—but I liked the idea of this family going out and trying to find their way in the world."

Ford's good-looking elder brother Francis (1881–1953) quickly established himself in Hollywood as an actor and director. Thanks to his influence, John (already and forever called "Jack" by his intimates) traveled to Los Angeles soon after leaving high school, and he found work as a propman and set laborer. For some years he stood in his brother's overweening shadow. He would double for Francis in various films, and he was hired as a Ku Klux Klan rider in D. W. Griffith's epic *The Birth of a Nation* (1915).

In 1917, thanks to his brother's persuasive influence on producer Carl Laemmle, Ford made his debut as a director with a two-reel Western, *The Tornado*. By 1920 he had some thirty films to his credit, mostly Westerns, for Laemmle's studio, Universal. Most have been lost to fire and negligence, although *Straight Shooting* (1917), his first feature, has been restored—and it demonstrates Ford's precocious skills as a director of films on location. In 1921, Ford moved to Fox, where he would direct many of the films that established his reputation during the next twenty years: *The Iron Horse, Steamboat Round the Bend, The Prisoner of Shark Island, Young Mr. Lincoln, Drums Along the Mohawk*, and *The Grapes of Wrath*. Ford, as prolific as any of his contemporaries, also worked for other studios, such as RKO (*The Lost Patrol, The Informer, Mary of Scotland, The Plough and the Stars*), MGM (*Flesh*), Samuel Goldwyn and United Artists (*Arrowsmith, The Hurricane*), and Columbia (*The Whole Town's Talking*).

By the time he made *Stagecoach* in 1939, Ford's Western career appeared to lie far away in his youth, but that film's unexpected triumph opened a new phase in his career. During World War II, Ford served his country with distinction as head of the Field Photographic Branch of the Office of Strategic Services (OSS). His unit made numerous documentaries, some of which he photographed himself in hazardous conditions (notably *The Battle of Midway*).

From 1945 on, Ford pursued an eclectic course, traveling here, there, and everywhere for his subjects, whether it was to Mexico for *The Fugitive* (1947), to Ireland for *The Quiet Man* (1952), to Africa for *Mogambo* (1953), to Britain for *Gideon of Scotland Yard* (1959), or to Hawaii for *Donovan's Reef* (1963). But his preferred location remained Monument Valley, and the Westerns he made there are discussed in this book.

John Ford died in 1973, honored by his industry as perhaps the most distinguished American director of the first seventy-five years of cinema. When Orson Welles was asked whom he admired most among filmmakers, he responded: "The old masters. By which I mean John Ford, John Ford, and John Ford."

John Ford (right) on location for *Donovan's Reef* in 1963

Ford and his crew prepare a shot for *Cheyenne Autumn* just below "John Ford Point"

CHAPTER 1

THE MYTH OF THE WEST

Texas, 1868. An instant of darkness. Then a woman draws open a door and the camera accompanies her, slyly, into sunlight. Shielding her eyes against the glare of a cyan sky, she locates a movement in the desert scrub. A caped horseman emerges from the primeval floor of Monument Valley. John Wayne, alias Ethan Edwards, has returned. . . .

These opening shots of John Ford's 1956 masterpiece, *The Searchers,* embody the romance and myth of the Western movie. Two elements prevail in this first scene: the cherished quality of kinship in alien surroundings, and the stilled tumult of the landscape itself. Ford's films rarely err on the side of realism; rather they present us with a mythic vision of the plains and deserts of the American West, embodied most memorably in Monument Valley, with its buttes and mesas that tower above the men on horseback, whether they be settlers, soldiers, or Native Americans. Fellow director Anthony Mann's great suite of Westerns, made during the 1950s, espouse the same pioneering vision of a Land of Milk and Honey, but Mann's settlers must struggle over the high mountains and become as wily and vicious as the villains—usually white men—who impede their progress.

John Ford made some fifty Westerns during a career that spanned almost six decades. Many of these have entered movie history as imperishable examples of the Western spirit: *The Iron Horse, Stagecoach, My Darling Clementine, Fort Apache, She Wore a Yellow Ribbon, Rio Grande, Wagon Master,* and *The Searchers.*

His best work unfolds at the interface between old and new, between the traditional Indian way of life and the inexorable tide of civilization. His heroes tend to be outsiders, even rejects from society, men who served in the Civil War and men who cherish a tear-tinged memory of a West where human dignity and family values held sway. More often than not, they are played by stalwarts of the genre such as John Wayne, Henry Fonda, and Richard Widmark. His richest sequences, such as the open-air dance in *My Darling Clementine,* or the reconciliation between father and son in *Rio Grande,* breathe with an unrivaled intensity and simplicity of emotion.

Although restricted to black-and-white cinematography for most of his career, Ford proved that a monochrome sky could be as lyrical as a blue horizon. His color films set new benchmarks for imaginative rendering of the Great Outdoors, with the mysterious umber and flaming vermilion of Arizona contrasting with the yellow scarves and blue uniforms of the troopers crossing the skyline. Ford could also evoke both the vanished world of the American Revolution along New York's western frontier, in the early masterpiece *Drums Along the Mohawk,* and the pre–Civil War innocence of *Young Mr. Lincoln.*

Ford's Westerns emerge not so much from historical reality as from an ideal that blends love of family with a pioneering spirit. The inspiration for that ideal flows in part from the director's Irish roots. Ford's greatest works in the genre show settlers and cattlemen at the mercy of elements and Indians alike. This sense of vulnerability in the face of an untamed environment stems from the journals of Lewis and Clark (written between 1804 and 1806) and was given pictorial resonance by the painters and illustrators of the late nineteenth and early twentieth centuries.

The ideal, or rather the myth, of the American West goes back even further in time. As Philippe Fraisse has written, "The Far West is not America, any more than Ilium was Greece." To the early-nineteenth-century American, anywhere beyond the Ohio Valley and the Mississippi River loomed as wilderness, uncharted and fraught with peril. Native Americans, lurking in forest and canyon alike, were regarded as dangerous vermin. Frederick Jackson Turner, writing in 1893, noted: "One of the most striking phases of frontier adjustment, was the proposal of the Rev. Solomon Stoddard of Northampton in the fall of 1703, urging the use of dogs 'to hunt Indians as they do Bears.' The argument was that the dogs would catch many an Indian who would be too light of foot for the townsmen, nor was it thought of as inhuman; for the Indians 'act like wolves and are to be dealt with as wolves.'" Almost a full century of what Turner called "Indian fighting and forest felling" was needed to advance the colonial settlements a mere hundred miles westward from the eastern seaboard.

Between 1754 and 1763, France and Great Britain were locked in a struggle for control of the colonial territory of North America. It is a subject Ford tackled with obvious relish in *Drums Along the Mohawk* (1939). Turner wrote that during that period, "The forested region of [the Midwest] was occupied by the wigwams of many different tribes of the Algonquin tongue, sparsely scattered in villages along the water courses, warring and trading through the vast wilderness. The western edge of the prairie and the Great Plains were held by the Sioux, chasing herds of bison across these far-stretching expanses." Even half a century later, when Jefferson purchased what amounted to most of the land west of the Mississippi River from Napoleon for a mere twenty-seven million dollars (including interest!), the pioneers had, according to Turner, "hardly more than entered the outskirts of the forest along the Ohio and Lake Erie."

James Fenimore Cooper's ebullient leading character, Natty Bumppo, alias "Leatherstocking," first surfaced as an old man in *The Pioneers* (published in 1823), but three years later he could be found in the prime of life in *The Last of the Mohicans,* the novelist's immortal tale of the Franco-British war, when the Native Americans were at once courted and reviled as each side acknowledged their significance as allies. The irony is that, although dismissed as savages by the white colonialists, the Indians learned a trick or two from their invaders. "I should point out," declared the veteran actor Iron Eyes Cody in his memoirs, "that the French were the first to introduce scalping to the New World."

Selling in startling numbers, the novels of Cooper persuaded an entire generation of Americans that "God's Wilderness," as Leatherstocking termed it, lay just over the horizon. Documentary evidence had begun to support such a vision. The journals of Lewis and Clark, Francis Parkman's *The Oregon Trail* (1849), and the palette of painters such as George Catlin, Seth Eastman, and Thomas Cole entranced any number of cultivated Americans. The majestic wilderness bore overtones of bounty and danger in equal measure. As Hamlin Garland would write later in the century, "Long before the days of '49, the West had become the Golden West, the land of wealth and freedom and happiness. All of the associations called up by the spoken word, the West, were fabulous, mythic, hopeful." Most of the brooding landscapes of Cole and his younger contemporaries Jasper Francis Cropsey and John Frederick Kensett depict nothing more remote than the Catskills of upstate New York or the White Mountains of New Hampshire. But the absence of human habitation and the awesome, almost sinister power of nature, as exemplified in storm clouds and torrential rains, strengthen the image of a wilderness still to be won.

George Caleb Bingham's painting *The Emigration of Daniel Boone* (1851) shows the famous Kentuckian leading a number of settlers with wives, children, and livestock out into what Henry Nash Smith called "a dreamily beautiful wilderness which they obviously meant to bring under the plow." Timothy Flint, Boone's most celebrated early biographer, wrote that the pioneer "delighted in the thought that 'the rich and boundless valleys of the great west—the garden of the earth—and the paradise of hunters, had been won from the dominion of the savage tribes, and opened as an asylum for the oppressed, the enterprising, and the free of every land.'"

Henry David Thoreau, author of the *Walden* essays, asserted that to the east lay the city, to the west the wilderness, "and ever I am leaving the city more and more, and withdrawing into the wilderness"—even if that "wilderness" in his case was in the proximity of Concord, Massachusetts, hardly yet the Great Plains or the Rockies.

Henry Nash Smith reminds us that "the existence of an uninhabitable desert east of the Rocky Mountains had first been announced to the American public in 1810, when Zebulon M. Pike published the journal of his expedition across the plains to the upper Rio Grande valley." Some thirty years later, Thomas J. Farnham, who trekked from Illinois to Oregon in 1839, wrote that "the Great American Desert," stretching three hundred miles east of the Rocky Mountains, was a scene of desolation, a "burnt and arid desert, whose solemn silence is seldom broken by the tread of any other animal than the wolf or the starved and thirsty horse which bears the traveller across its wastes."

Meanwhile, the opening of the Oregon Trail meant that frontier farmers could take their families overland toward the Pacific. In May 1843, about a thousand American families gathered with their wagons and provisions at the confluence of the Kansas and Missouri Rivers. According to the contemporary writer William Gilpin, "This hardy band, accompanied by 122 wagons, in the short space of five months penetrated to the Pacific, opening and traveling along a road of 1,000 miles of plains and 1,500 of vast mountains . . . without other guide than an indomitable perseverance, or other protection than their invincible rifles, and their wives and progeny clustered around them."

Francis Parkman, among the greatest of the nineteenth-century travel writers, described the migrants preparing for nightfall: "The wagons, some fifty in number, with here and there a tent intervening, were arranged as usual in a circle; in the area within, the best horses were picketed, and the whole circumference was glowing with the dusky light of the fires, displaying the forms of the women and children who were crowded around them."

The movement westward accelerated, literally, to a rush in 1848 when gold was discovered in California, and in 1859 when silver as well as gold surfaced in Nevada and Colorado. Neophyte prospectors hastened as far west as Alaska and Oregon in their quest for a stake in what promised to be unlimited wealth. Even in the late 1840s, Parkman also reported seeing the white wagons of Mormon pilgrims on the trail toward their promised land of Utah, a theme that Ford would develop in his most underrated Western, *Wagon Master* (1950). In 1859, Horace Greeley, founder of the *New York Tribune,* uttered his celebrated rallying cry: "Go West, young man, and grow up with the country!"

Two events transformed America in the 1860s and also furnished John Ford with some of his richest material: the Civil War and the completion of the transcontinental railroad. Both were recorded by photographers, introducing a fresh, and more realistic, view of contemporary history. Mathew Brady's portraits of the rich and famous brought him renown even before the Civil War, which he covered with opportunistic gusto, deploying a bevy of photographers to take pictures of the various troops and engagements. In the early 1860s, Brady achieved notoriety with his photographs of "the dead of Antietam." Faced with such ghastly naturalism, the *New York Times* commented that Brady had brought "home to us the terrible reality and earnestness of war." Ford was intrigued less by the war as such than by its aftermath—the convulsive effect on survivors of both North and South, the spirit of the Seventh Cavalry, the nostalgia for some elusive graciousness of life in the antebellum South, and an unspoken humility in the minds of officers who had seen such carnage and knew then that the Indian was not the only savage on the continent.

Alexander Gardner (1821–1882), who was chief photographer for the eastern division of the Union Pacific Railroad, produced many of the images that inspired Ford in *The Iron Horse* (1924). The challenge of crossing, or penetrating, first the Rockies and then the High Sierra fascinated a generation of Americans. But Native Americans looked on the building of the railroad as a mortal development, rendering the horse, however fleet of foot, redundant.

By 1901, Vice President Theodore Roosevelt could assert, "The conquest and settlement of the West . . . has been the stupendous feat of our race for the century that has just closed. . . . It is a record of men who greatly dared and greatly did; a record of wanderings wider and more dangerous than those of the Vikings; a record of endless feats of arms, of victory after victory in the ceaseless strife waged against wild man and wild nature. The winning of the West was the great epic feat in the history of our race."

This idealized image of the American West, verging at times on the sentimental, can also be found in the paintings of Charles M. Russell (1865–1926) and Frederic Remington (1861–1909), the "titans of Western art." Gazing back at the nineteenth century from the perspective of the early years of the twentieth, Remington in particular joined Ford in celebrating the Native American as Noble Savage and the cowboy as the quintessential frontiersman, enveloped in a landscape at once menacing and magnificent.

Remington grew up in the years when the reputation of the German-born painter Albert Bierstadt (1830–1902) was gathering enormous momentum. During the 1860s, Bierstadt contributed the most spectacular images of this Western utopia—a place of mighty gorges and rushing rivers, resplendent in its primeval purity and not yet spoiled by the greedy artifacts of human civilization. Both *Looking Down Yosemite Valley* (opposite, top) and *Yosemite Valley* (1868) embody Bierstadt's eye for the expansive, immutable landscape, and they also remind the avid moviegoer of Ford's Monument Valley compositions. In the great preponderance of Bierstadt's compositions, one finds the contrast between lush green valley floors and the soaring nobility of the surrounding mountains. In *Looking Down Yosemite Valley* and *Mount Whitney* (opposite, bottom), an almost blinding sun predominates in the distance, like the blessing over a promised land. The audacity of Bierstadt's compositions, and his readiness to depart from naturalism in order to achieve grandeur, gave regions such as Yosemite the dimensions of an almost Keatsian paradise. One critic said of *Looking Down Yosemite Valley*: "It looks as if it was painted in an Eldorado, in a distant land of gold, heard of in a song and story; dreamed of but never seen."

If Bierstadt's use of space and light recall that of his fellow German painter Caspar David Friedrich, then the luxuriant paintings of Thomas Moran (1837–1926) hark back to an English heritage, in particular to J. M. W. Turner (1775–1851). Turner's *Apollo and Python* (1811) clearly influenced Moran's spectacular canvas *Hiawatha and the Great Serpent, the Kenabeek* (1867), with its sun-bathed summits soaring above the somber waters where Hiawatha draws his mighty bow of ash in defiance of the writhing serpents confronting him.

Four years later, Moran traveled through the western United States with a young photographer named William Henry Jackson (1843–1942). While Moran made

Albert Bierstadt. *Looking Down Yosemite Valley*. 1865. Oil on canvas, 64 x 96¼". Birmingham Museum of Art, Alabama. Gift of the Birmingham Public Library

Albert Bierstadt. *Mount Whitney*. c. 1877. Oil on canvas, 68⅞ x 116⅝". Rockwell Museum of Western Art, Corning, New York

sketches for his views of the bluffs and towers in the prevailing desert, Jackson took hundreds of photographs that were subsequently reproduced by the Detroit Publishing Company in the form of tinted postcards and sold in the tens of thousands, promoting the image of the West as an Eden-in-waiting. Moran, however, focused on the fantasy of the Far West, rather than its precise contours. "I place no value upon literal transcripts from Nature," he maintained. "My general scope is not realistic; all my tendencies are towards idealization."

His *Green River* (below) endows the Wyoming landscape with a grandeur of near-mythic proportions. Horsemen have penetrated the region, but they are dwarfed by the colossal, serried phalanx of mountains, bathed in a golden halo of light. In *Nearing Camp, Evening on the Upper Colorado River, Wyoming* (1882), Moran renders the huge volcanic buttes beyond the river in much the same way as Ford would do with his Monument Valley horizons. And he includes a group of Indians on horseback, en route to a camp on the river's floodplain—something that was conceivable, if implausible, in the early 1880s, by which time the Indians had mostly been evicted from such regions. Andrew Wilton, who curated the

magnificent show *American Sublime* in 2002, pointed out Moran's affection for the Egyptian paintings of David Roberts, and he says that in *Nearing Camp,* "Moran evokes parallels between the wild spaces of Western America and the historically suggestive regions that Roberts had appropriated. The Green River buttes become an equivalent for the Pyramids, and the mountains of Colorado and Utah an American Moab or Arabia." Such a comment could as well be applied to Ford's use of Monument Valley in his Westerns.

The legacy of Turner also affected the work of the young Remington, which tends toward often shapeless landscapes, communicated in swath-strokes of yellow and green, thus forcing the viewer's eye to the physical action and figures that dominate the canvas. The everyday life of cattlemen, the exploits of soldiers in the wake of the Civil War, and the Native Americans scouring the plains for buffalo were all grist for his mill.

Remington, the son of a cavalry officer in the Civil War, adored the military uniforms of his youth, and he remembered to his dying day the impact of George Armstrong Custer's disastrous defeat in 1876, when Remington was just fourteen and about to enter the Highland Military Academy in Worcester, Massachusetts. Remington began sketching at an early age, drawing soldiers from every kind of regiment and army. His work reflects the pride of a white race flinging itself against the Native American, rejoicing in the challenge and relishing the inhospitable nature of the terrain. His dramatic imagery gives visual texture to a West described by Francis Parkman in his historical works, by Owen Wister in his fiction, and by Theodore Roosevelt in his speeches and articles. "I am working for big effects," Remington declared. "I am trying to picture the West as I saw it, big and full of color. I can't do it any other way."

Remington, like his contemporary Charles M. Russell, was enthralled by the finality of the conflict between whites and Native Americans. This explains the romantic nature of many of Remington's paintings and bronzes. His men, such as *The Arizona Cowboy* (page 24), are alone and heroic in a landscape that is only vaguely delineated.

Proficient at ranching, scouting, and trapping, Remington would recall in 1905: "I knew the wild riders and the vacant land were about to vanish forever . . . and the more I considered the subject, the bigger the forever loomed. Without knowing how to do it, I began to record some facts around me, and the more I looked the more the panorama unfolded." He became obsessed with accuracy, down to the tiniest detail, while always espousing an Impressionist technique. He would decide on one dominant color, applying the paint thickly and boldly, letting the action in each subject develop around that single hue—for example, the glaring white of the snow in *The Fall of the Cowboy* (page 26), or the blue sky that almost collides with the hot pink of the desert below in *The Sentinel* (c. 1907).

The instant, more than the implication, mattered to him. As a journalist dashes down the gist of an incident, so Remington would seize the essential lineaments of soldiers ready for battle, or a horse bucking its rider. Remington rarely depicted soldiers and Indians in face-to-face combat, as if he respected each side too much to chart its destruction. He remained loyal not just to the wilderness landscape, but also to the passionate human beings who stalked and rode among them, a quality that must have appealed to Ford. Remington's close friend (and later the president) Theodore Roosevelt sallied into the wilds with his own team of photographers, establishing "a very recognizable iconography of river bend, cattle on sand-bars, mid-day meals, the corral, high noon, captured thieves, Deadwood and so on." When Roosevelt penned his memoirs of ranch life in 1888, he asked Remington to provide the illustrations.

Both Remington and Russell echo in their visual work the exciting image of the West in dime novels and popular plays—a place filled with galloping horses, blazing six-guns, and dramatic ambushes. However, Russell disliked the military uniforms and traditions so beloved of Remington. Russell's hometown was St. Louis, where he was exposed to the paintings of Carl Wimar and other artists of the early nineteenth century. A nomad by nature, Russell began working on ranches in Montana and elsewhere at the age of seventeen. Wrangling, roping, and riding, he

Frederic Remington. *The Arizona Cowboy.* 1901. Pastel and graphite on paper, 30 x 24". Rockwell Museum of Western Art, Corning, New York

OPPOSITE
Henry Fonda in *My Darling Clementine,* viewed from the desert scrub to make him dominate even Mitchell Butte in Monument Valley

took part in numerous cattle drives. Between 1882 and 1892, he spent every spring and autumn in the roundup. At day's end he would sketch and paint his impressions of the cowboy culture changing around him. Russell also earned the trust of the Blackfoot Indians in southern Canada, and at intervals he would live among them, observing their customs. His breakthrough as an artist came in 1887, when a

Frederic S. Remington. *The Fall of the Cowboy*. 1895. Oil on canvas, 25 x 35⅛". Amon Carter Museum, Fort Worth, Texas

small watercolor entitled *Waiting for a Chinook* attracted the public. The grim composition shows a starving cow surrounded by wolves, a metaphor for the impending disappearance of the open-range cattle industry that had so impressed the artist. Russell's distinctive signature—the outline of a buffalo skull—symbolized the death of a way of life.

Extraordinarily prolific, Russell produced some twenty-five hundred paintings, drawings, and sketches. Like Ford, Russell was an imaginative observer, treating fantasy in a matter-of-fact idiom, and he excited viewers with pictures such as *Indians Hunting Buffalo* (1894) and *Wounded (The Wounded Buffalo)* (1909). And as with Ford, a bass current of humor runs through Russell's best work—*Cow Punching Sometimes Spells Trouble* (1889) exemplifies this trait, as does *A Quiet Day in Utica* (page 28), with the dogs and ducks scattering in the wake of a posse of riders. Russell gave equal attention to cowboy and Indian, accentuating the essential pride and dignity of both. *The Scout* (page 29), in particular, involves a subtle interplay of natural colors, with the sky brooding behind the haughty warrior.

Ford's brother Francis knew Russell and, with Jack, would meet the artist at Harry Carey's ranch on various occasions. From both Russell and Remington, observes Joseph McBride, "Ford learned the paradoxical method of capturing the grittiness of frontier life and landscapes in moments of intensely romantic, often statuesque beauty."

As settlers began to take advantage of the railroad traversing the nation, so the images of the West as a Keatsian "faery land forlorn" began to recede in favor of a transplanted microcosm of family life back East. Schools were built, churches were dedicated (as Ford depicts in *My Darling Clementine*), children grew up knowing no environment other than the dusty plains and the soaring Rockies. By 1880, Frederick Jackson Turner asserted, settlements had taken permanent root in northern Michigan, Wisconsin, and Minnesota, along the Dakota rivers, and in the Black Hills region. The frontier, dividing civilization from what whites perceived as a state of savagery, could be safely located in the ranches and mining camps of the Great Plains and Colorado, Montana, and Idaho. The lithographs of Currier and

Charles M. Russell.
A Quiet Day in Utica.
1907. Oil on canvas,
24⅛ x 36⅛". Courtesy
Sid Richardson
Collection of Western
Art, Fort Worth, Texas

Charles M. Russell.
The Scout. 1907. Pencil,
watercolor, and
gouache on paper,
16¾ x 11⅜". Courtesy
Sid Richardson
Collection of Western
Art, Fort Worth, Texas

Henry Farny. *The Sign of Peace*. 1908. Oil on canvas, 40¼ x 22¼". Rockwell Museum of Western Art, Corning, New York

Ives helped to popularize this migration, but artists of the period, like filmmakers half a century later, concentrated their talents on masculine exploits—cowboys, Indian warriors, and of course the U.S. Cavalry and its courageous scouts.

David M. Emmons has argued that "the myth of the West was . . . a production, as surely as were the tons of steel ingots and the miles of cotton cloth, of a market driven industrializing society. It gave to the dominant elements of that society—mostly eastern—a powerful argument against those who challenged their dominance."

Some painters dwelled exclusively on the North American Indian. Perhaps the earliest was George Catlin (1796–1872), who eschewed violence and blood in favor of an ethnographic image of Native Americans—Sioux, Fox, and Sauk in particular, dressed in traditional costume and posing for portraits. Seth Eastman (1809–1875) also brought a shrewd and perceptive eye to bear on Indian customs, and a generation later Henry Farny (1847–1916) made sketches and took photographs of Indians he encountered on his journeys west in the 1880s. He would accumulate artifacts on his travels and bring them back to his studio to add verisimilitude to such canvases as *The Song of the Talking Wire* (1904). In *The Sign of Peace* (opposite), Farny gives his Indian tribesman a relaxed, contained splendor, the upraised right hand signaling authority as well as peace, and the absence of weapons symbolizing the wish to live in harmony with the white man.

Among the most dynamic of all Western painters was Charles C. Schreyvogel (1861–1912). Ford's son recalled that the director kept a copy of a collection of Schreyvogel's works beside his bed: "He pored over it to dream up action sequences for his films." At first, Schreyvogel "practiced" by painting the Native Americans on view in Buffalo Bill's Wild West shows, but in 1893 he trekked to the Ute reservation in Colorado. Like Farny, he retrieved Indian artifacts and costumes to give him inspiration while seated before his easel in the comfort of his home in Hoboken, New Jersey. His sense of drama, and his flair for creating movement within a composition, soon brought him acclaim. In *An Unexpected Enemy* (page 32), Schreyvogel concentrates a palpable degree of energy as the riderless horse gallops toward the viewer and the two troopers level their weapons at an approaching

Charles C. Schreyvogel. *An Unexpected Enemy.* 1900. Oil on canvas, 33¾ x 24¾". Rockwell Museum of Western Art, Corning, New York

bear. Ford may have paid tribute to Schreyvogel's *My Bunkie* (1900) in *Rio Grande* (1950), in a scene depicting a cavalry rider pulling up a wounded colleague onto his galloping horse.

The gulf between fact and fiction in Western life was accentuated almost more by words than by pictures. Huge numbers of dime novels were published, amounting to several thousand titles by the close of the nineteenth century, most of which portrayed the valiant white hunter slaughtering Indians by the score. James Fenimore Cooper's Leatherstocking now appeared tame by comparison with Buffalo Bill Cody in *The King of the Border Men,* which the editors of the *New York Weekly* dubbed "The Greatest Romance of the Age!" By 1878 at the latest, one Prentiss Ingraham, an inveterate dime novelist, had in effect become a staff writer for Cody, portraying Buffalo Bill as "one of America's strange heroes who has loved the trackless wilds, rolling plains and mountain solitudes of our land, far more than the bustle and turmoil, the busy life and joys of our cities, and who has stood as a barrier between civilization and savagery, risking his own life to save the lives of others."

Ford grew up nourished by stories of the West less evanescent than the dime novel. Like many another teenager of the period, he devoured the novels of Cooper, Bret Harte, and Mark Twain. Nostalgia tinted almost everything he read and saw. The West appealed to him as a theater in which such family allegiances could both prosper and be tested (page 34). One thinks of Wyatt Earp burying his younger brother James in the desert outside Tombstone in *My Darling Clementine*, then visiting the grave with his surviving brothers as often as possible.

The settlement of the West, along with the ravaging of Indian civilization, was justified in the name of the family and its values. In Ford's work, characters from "back East" arrived with heavy metaphorical baggage—whether it be Doc Holliday with his Ivy League education in *My Darling Clementine,* or the duplicitous Gatewood in *Stagecoach,* or indeed the demure, virginal women who descend from many a stagecoach. In the words of Frederick Jackson Turner in 1896, "In spite of his rude, gross nature, this early Western man was an idealist withal. He dreamed dreams

OPPOSITE
The family unit before disaster strikes in *The Searchers*. From left to right: Walter Coy, Pippa Scott, Robert Lydon, Lana Wood, John Wayne, and Dorothy Jordan

and beheld visions. He had faith in man, hope for democracy, belief in America's destiny, unbounded confidence in his ability to make his dreams come true."

John Ford, like Remington more than half a century earlier, would create "a reality of his own that became reality for others." He not only would develop a vision of the Old West (a "West," moreover, that had only receded into legend in the years following Ford's own birth), but he also would interpret specific features of American history—such as the building of the railroads, Abraham Lincoln's youth (and, in *The Prisoner of Shark Island*, his assassination), and the Civil War—in as realistic a way as possible.

John Ford in younger days

The Iron Horse: Filming
within a film—the
joining of the Union
Pacific and Central

CHAPTER 2

HISTORY TRANSFIGURED

The gold rush interested Anthony Mann more than it did John Ford, and Mann films such as *The Far Country, Bend of the River,* and *The Man from Laramie* exemplify the atmosphere of violence and avarice that colored the period.

Ford responded to another kind of precious commodity—cattle—in *My Darling Clementine,* just as Howard Hawks did in *Red River.* The cattleman, seeing the homesteader as someone who took the cattle's grass to feed sheep, set out to evict him. Both factions were part of the broad westward movement that profoundly reshaped the nation during the nineteenth century. This movement is reflected in paintings such as Albert Bierstadt's *Surveyor's Wagon in the Rockies* (see page 68), which dates from 1859, only a decade after the gold rush accelerated that migration. Although the mules appear tame by comparison with the horses traditionally attached to such wagons, the painting communicates the contrast between the yellow-flowering sagebrush of the plain and the distant challenge of the mountains.

Perhaps not even the assassination of Abraham Lincoln had as long lasting an impact on American life as did the joining of the Union Pacific and Central Pacific Railroads at Promontory Point, Utah, in 1869. The image of the "iron horse," which connected the east and west coasts of the continent with a power that swept away the horse and the stagecoach, continued to impress artists more than a century later, as the Native American Carm Little Turtle's hand-painted photo montage *Iron Horse* indicates (opposite).

The Iron Horse, made in 1924, was already John Ford's fiftieth film, and it pulsates with the self-confidence of a man who knew how to film in the great outdoors and whose knowledge of human nature was increasing by the month. His uncle Mike had worked on the construction of the Union Pacific, Ford noted: "He told me stories about it and taught me the songs they had sung. I was always interested in the railroad and wanted to make a picture about it."

Ford determined to render the story with as much historical accuracy as he could muster, and one of the opening titles in *The Iron Horse* asserts that the film is "accurate and faithful in every particular." By the 1860s, photography was close to replacing painting as the principal means of disseminating images. Mathew Brady's team of cameramen had captured harrowing moments from the Civil War, and the completion of the transcontinental railroad enterprise was photographed by men like Alexander Gardner. Ford studied these photos, and the filmed scenes set at Promontory Point represent the tableaux that were caught on camera at the time (page 36).

The Iron Horse ranks with D. W. Griffith's major works as one of the great epics of the silent cinema. Shot almost entirely on location (apart from an obviously painted backdrop of a canyon), it enabled Ford to escape from Hollywood and work with hundreds of different people in spectacular surroundings. An earlier Ford Western, *The Ace of the Saddle* (1919), had been shot in the Rio Grande valley, but *The Iron Horse* proved an altogether more formidable enterprise, featuring 1,280 separate scenes. One hundred cooks were required to feed the five thousand extras involved. The budget ran to $280,000, and the film went on to earn an impressive $2 million at the box office. Sets representing the two major frontier

Carm Little Turtle.
Iron Horse. 1990/2000.
Sepia-toned print with
oils, 8½ x 12½".
Rockwell Museum of
Western Art, Corning,
New York

towns featured in the story, North Platte, Nebraska, and Cheyenne, Wyoming, were built by Ford's crew at Dodge Flats, Nevada, near a spur of track being built by the Southern Pacific Railroad.

Harold Schuster worked on *The Iron Horse* as an assistant editor and actor, and he later described it to Kevin Brownlow: "In the distance, I could see a Western town, mostly tents, and a few shacks. It represented North Platte, and later, with changes, it became Cheyenne and other towns that mushroomed and decayed as the rail-laying moved forward. I remember the Indian tepees encamped on the left of the town towards the mountains. They were the real thing, and the various nations brought their own" (opposite). Nor were they alone: some thirty Chinese workers and unskilled laborers joined the team, an indication of the insufficient white labor in the West. Ford's inter-titles also refer to the railroads' recruitment of numerous former soldiers in the Civil War—from both sides—after it ended in 1865.

Property man Lefty Hough remembered: "Many things happened on that picture. The steward in the dining car died of pneumonia. We had a marriage. We had a carload of coal brought in and the Indians stole the coal. The cooks in the cook-house were selling big roasts to the Indians for fifteen cents. So we were running out of food. This is when the production man got fired. He was living in Reno in a whorehouse—which we could never find. We sent for the big boss of the studio, and he came up and fired him."

Improvising, injecting ad-libs wherever he could, Ford attacked the project with sustained gusto. He began to perfect his technique of letting the action occur within the frame, rather than repeatedly turning the camera like a nervous tic. He also fixed the camera to the front of a locomotive and loaded it aboard moving trucks, so that galloping Indians and other riders could be seen in much wider compositions than if just the camera had tracked alongside them. Cinematographer George Schneiderman filmed scenes of Indians milling around, and workers striking in protest, with a sternly static camera, thus producing an image of turbulence in depth. Although Monument Valley still lay beyond his ken, Ford had already devised memorable images: Indians massed on the crest of a hill; a small band of

Ford on horseback during the filming of *The Iron Horse*

riders vanishing into a dusty sunset. In one unforgettable shot, the shadows of Indian riders loom up on the side of the pay train they have ambushed. Toward the climax of the film, hundreds of Pawnee tribesmen flow across the water in increasingly impressionistic, almost abstract, imagery. Still, Ford did not reject the tracking shot when it suited him: for example, Indians pursue the trains at high speed, just as they would the vehicle in *Stagecoach* fifteen years later. And the final frenzy of track-laying is expressed with kinetic fluency and vibrancy.

Even if Ford seemed flushed by what one early inter-title calls "the momentum of a great nation pushing Westward," he refused to accept received opinion about Native American iniquity. The father of the film's hero is cut down near his campfire at night by Indians—but Indians led by a ruthless white renegade, who will become the villain of the story.

Still, *The Iron Horse* did perpetuate other legends of the West, for example in an inter-title that refers to Buffalo Bill Cody supplying buffalo meat to the men of the

The Iron Horse: Reunion for George O'Brien's Davy Brandon (second from left) and his Irish pals of yesteryear

Union Pacific Railroad. The cowboy thus assumed mythic, heroic proportions, while in reality he was often little more than a "herder," eating and sheltering as best he could while tending to mangy cattle and truculent horses. Ford would never quite contemplate this forbidding image, and it surfaced rarely in Hollywood Westerns until the likes of Tom Gries's *Will Penny* (1968) and Clint Eastwood's *Unforgiven* (1992).

Ford's least pretentious historical film, *Young Mr. Lincoln,* was made in that *annus mirabilis* of 1939, when the director also completed two other masterly pictures, *Stagecoach* and *Drums Along the Mohawk.* For Ford, Joseph McBride has written, "Lincoln is the archetypal figure of justice, a man who dispenses legal wisdom with a priestlike humor, charity, and tolerance."

The film opens with Lincoln (page 45), just twenty-three years of age, representing the Whig Party as a candidate for the legislature. The law beckons, and a reading of *Blackstone's Commentaries* beside the Sangamon River in New Salem, Illinois, convinces Lincoln of the fundamental distinction between right and wrong. By now accustomed to losing loved ones—his mother, his sister—Lincoln grieves at the sudden death of his sweetheart, Ann Rutledge, but presses ahead with his career. He travels to Springfield to go into partnership as a lawyer.

Before long, he finds himself defending two brothers accused of killing another man in a brawl. Lincoln reveals the obstinacy of purpose that would characterize his presidency, refusing to kowtow to either judge or prosecuting counsel—and then coming up with a marvelous *coup de théâtre* to expose Ward Bond's blustering witness John Palmer Cass as a liar and murderer. Screenwriter Lamar Trotti took this detail from the Duff Armstrong trial of 1857, when Lincoln proved his client's innocence by producing an almanac to demonstrate that there could not have been any moonlight at the hour of the crime. The filmmakers also, to judge from Carl Sandburg's classic biography, borrowed Lincoln's own comments when selecting jurors for that Beardstown trial: "Tell me, are you the son of . . . ? Well, you are a smart boy if you take after your dad."

Ford's Westerns revolve around close-knit communities where everyone knows everyone else, and idiosyncrasies abound. In *Young Mr. Lincoln,* Ford uses Springfield as a metaphor for the mighty nation that Lincoln would later preside over. The town boasted only 1,400 inhabitants in 1837—among them, Mary Todd, by all accounts a nimble dancer and attractive heiress (at least her father had been a senator and was president of the Bank of Kentucky). Ford sketches their first encounter with wit and wisdom, as at first they dance to the tune of "Oh, Dem Golden Slippers," when Lincoln cuts as awkward a figure as would Wyatt Earp in *My Darling Clementine* and Colonel Thursday in *Fort Apache*—and the rollicking melody would be the same. After they move out to the balcony, Mary tries to make small talk and then, sensibly, withdraws a few paces to observe the tongue-tied Lincoln with a compassionate eye.

Henry Fonda wore a false nose and a wart to stress his physical likeness to Lincoln, but Ford and Trotti also were at pains to show the future president's little flaws—cheating during a tug-of-war, for example, and boasting to Abigail Clay (mother of the accused brothers) that he can sink an ax deeper than anyone he knows. The fact remains that Lincoln in youth was keenly aware of his own physical strength, and Sandburg writes that he actually spoke (on an earlier occasion) the line in the film when, confronted by a lynch mob, he shouts: "I'm the big buck of this lick. If any of you want to try it, come on and whet your horns."

The film even pokes fun at the American pioneer myth, when the hectoring prosecutor claims that the murder victim was "an American, in whose veins flowed the blood of pioneers who braved the wilderness to make this great state what it is"—while Ford intercuts close-ups of the judge snoring away imperturbably.

Ford's own idiosyncrasies as a filmmaker give *Young Mr. Lincoln* a distinctive rhythm. Transitions from scene to scene are both abrupt and eloquent—for example, the sudden revelation of Ann's death, with Lincoln visiting her grave beside a river swollen with winter ice. Such aesthetic decisions do not undermine the historical verisimilitude of the film, with its mood of Manifest Destiny in an America not yet wracked by civil war. *Young Mr. Lincoln* concludes on a note of subdued apotheosis, hinting at the greatness of the man that would emerge from his experiences in Springfield.

Filming *Young Mr. Lincoln:* Ford is in the lower foreground, wearing a black beret.

Henry Fonda

Although John Wayne starred in John Ford's first great Western, *Stagecoach,* Henry Fonda (1905–1982) had established himself by then as the director's favorite screen personality. Fonda was certainly not launched to stardom by Ford, who chose him for three films in the space of eighteen months in 1939–40: *Young Mr. Lincoln, Drums Along the Mohawk,* and *The Grapes of Wrath*. Chameleon-like, he assumes a distinctive look in each picture. For Abraham Lincoln, he wore his hair full and wavy, emphasizing the angular drop of his face. For farmer Gil Martin (opposite), he sported a pigtail. And for Tom Joad, a bulky cap only underlined the severity of his clear-eyed gaze. In all three films, Fonda embodied an immaculate integrity and nobility of purpose.

In the opening sequences of *Young Mr. Lincoln,* with Abe in New Salem in 1832, Fonda's lanky, stretching gait is already apparent. He wears his stovepipe hat as though to the manor born (page 48). He plays traditional folk tunes on his Jew's harp, eager to be alone with his thoughts. He's an expert splitter of logs, and he brings the solemnity of a Solomon to a local pie-judging contest. Fonda's greatest moment comes not at the climax of the protracted murder trial against Matt and Adam Clay, but earlier, when he defuses the fury of a mob bent on lynching the brothers. Fonda has no need of invective, or the usual harangue. He relies on homespun eloquence, the voice of reason that brings a hush to the town square. As Lincoln stands foursquare against the door of the jail, the men lay down their battering ram with wonderful expressiveness—relief mingled with shame at the recognition of their animal self.

Fonda's eighteenth-century farmer in *Drums Along the Mohawk* is an altogether more vulnerable individual. Beneath his courage in joining the militia to fight the Indians and the British, there dwells a palpable fear of losing not just his own life but also those of his young wife and, soon, their child. When Joe Boleo (played by Ford's brother Francis) is caught and burned before he can reach a nearby fort for help, Gil runs off in his stead, loping through field and wood with that unmistakable stride of his, head and chest sloping down to challenge the wind.

Fonda's earnestness achieves its greatest moments in *The Grapes of Wrath*. Tom Joad, home on parole from the penitentiary, takes on the features of an Everyman, suffering with grace and a deeply etched gaze (see page 6), and every so often lashing out against exploitation.

Henry Fonda as Gil Martin in *Drums Along the Mohawk*

Fonda returned to Ford's cinema after World War II. In *My Darling Clementine,* his Wyatt Earp is the epitome of restraint. He wears a laconic, beaten look. His eyes house a hundred sorrows. He is a kind of reluctant deliverer, a chivalrous figure on horseback. Unruffled, supple, and catlike in the gunfight at the O.K. Corral, Fonda's at his best when in repose, phlegmatic at the poker table, and emanating a wistfulness that has no name (opposite). It was his idea to sit at ease outside the hotel and balance himself in his chair with one foot pressing against the upright post (page 50).

In both *My Darling Clementine* and *Fort Apache* (his final work for Ford, who left *Mister Roberts* shortly after the start of filming), Fonda's gifted with a mustache. The hirsute look diminishes the fresh-faced candor of an earlier decade, and in *Fort Apache* it accentuates the image of a man anxious to claim status, as well as to mask some hidden insecurity. His Lieutenant Colonel Owen Thursday's tight-assed

Young Mr. Lincoln: Henry Fonda in the title role, outside the courthouse in Springfield

The crowded saloon so beloved of Ford. Henry Fonda as Wyatt Earp relaxes at the card table in *My Darling Clementine*.

attitude toward the army makes him a class-conscious prig, and his failure to recall names makes it even more plain that he despises those around him. Thursday earns a measure of respect in the final analysis, if only because of his misguided courage in the face of annihilation. Falsely branding Captain Kirby York (John Wayne) a coward, he refuses his subordinate's challenge to a duel, instead ordering him to return to the supply train with young Lieutenant Michael O'Rourke (John Agar). It's a subtle moment, for one cannot help feeling that some instinct makes Thursday realize the end is near and O'Rourke, his daughter's suitor, should be saved.

Helped astride his horse by a baffled York, Thursday demands his officer's saber and then, extolling York to command the regiment, rides into the canyon to join his beleaguered troops—and die with honor. This last exchange between the two men seems in retrospect to have been a symbolic passing of the flame from Fonda to Wayne in Ford's Western world.

Henry Fonda, as Wyatt Earp, improvised this memorably nonchalant pose in *My Darling Clementine*.

Drums Along the Mohawk revealed for the first time how skillful Ford could be when shooting in color. Bert Glennon and Ray Rennahan, his cinematographers on the project, worked with the still-fledgling Technicolor and its consultant Natalie Kalmus to create a lush, tinted look for the outdoor sequences and a somber-hued tone for the interiors. William Faulkner may have contributed anonymously to the screenplay, but the film is a one-sided vision of eighteenth-century history. As a dramatic tale punctuated with violence and loss, it wears the contours of a Western—even though its West is in the Mohawk Valley, upper New York, in 1776, as the Revolutionary War is heating up. The verdant locations, however, belong to the Wasatch Mountains in Utah. As in Monument Valley, nature here predominates

Claudette Colbert and Henry Fonda in *Drums Along the Mohawk*

over its human inhabitants. When the young couple, Gilbert and Magdalena (page 51), are married in Albany at the start of the film, the minister prays for them to "go forth into the wilderness to make a new home." Gil's single wagon, with the indispensable cow wandering along in tow as Alfred Newman's poignant score plays on the soundtrack, takes on the dimensions of an ark as it crosses the isolated skyline toward Gil and Lana's future home in Deerfield.

Meanwhile, the English Tories have been seeking to engage the local Indian tribes on their side, urging them to destroy the colonists' crops and cabins and to seize the white man's territory. Ford conveniently ignores the fact that the Iroquois had inhabited the land long before the colonists arrived. Much earlier, the Dutch had helped to corrupt the Mohawk, part of the Iroquois League, by plying them with firearms in exchange for beaver skins. By the mid-eighteenth century, the Mohawk population had shrunk steadily, and their traditional peaceful approach to life—propounded by the legendary Indian leader Hiawatha—had changed.

Ford brings alive a gallery of eccentric characters, all wedded to the wilderness and its promise of crops and prosperity. When the Mohawk burn Gil's humble home and fields (opposite), he and his wife take work for an aristocratic British widow, Mrs. McKlennar, played with gusto by Edna May Oliver. As the film progresses, and as more men are lost or wounded in the struggle against the Indians and the English, she becomes a mother figure, related in heart if not in accent to such great Fordian personalities as Ma Joad in *The Grapes of Wrath* and Kathleen York in *Rio Grande*. When Indians invade her house (page 54), she clings obdurately to her family bed and treats her foes with an engaging blend of derision and consternation, as if unable to contemplate that war can obliterate a dream.

If the character of Mrs. McKlennar verges on caricature, so does that of the feisty minister played by one of Ford's favorite Irish actors, Arthur Shields, while Ward Bond's Adam Hartman is nothing more than doltish. Even Claudette Colbert's bride evokes the blonde, blue-eyed heroine Alice Munro in *Last of the Mohicans,* cringing at the mercy of the wilderness and its savages. Chief John Big Tree's Blue Back appears as impassive as Buster Keaton—and almost as amusing—but he hardly qualifies as a freethinking Mohawk. When he raises a final laugh by

Indians burn and pillage the settlers' farm, in *Drums Along the Mohawk*.

The raid on Mrs. McKlennar's home in *Drums Along the Mohawk*

brandishing the eye patch of the treacherous Englishman (John Carradine) who has been stirring up the Indians, he becomes, in the words of Joseph McBride, "accepted by the whites as a sort of domesticated pet."

To some degree, this thin line between the entertaining and the absurd has a parallel in the struggle between life and death in the narrative course of the film. An American general needs his leg to be amputated—and dies when an inexperienced doctor cannot stop the bleeding. The widow succumbs to a gunshot fired almost by accident, and Gil himself only just manages to struggle back after a gruesome engagement. The birth of Lana's child, however, provokes a stirring barn dance of the kind that in *My Darling Clementine* and *The Searchers* would become a trademark of Ford's Westerns.

The overriding sentiment sustaining *Drums Along the Mohawk* remains that of the defense of "God's country," comparable in its passion with the quest for the fabled Northwest Passage. The pictorial style of the film bears this out. When Gil's cabin in Deerfield (built, we are told, with his own hands) is overwhelmed by the Indians beneath a bright blue sky, the sense of violation is more vivid than it would have been in monochrome. Henry Nash Smith claimed that the image of "this vast and constantly-growing agricultural society in the interior of the continent became one of the dominant symbols of nineteenth-century American society—a collective representation, a poetic idea . . . that defined the promise of American life." Ford always identified with the colonists and settlers, remembering perhaps how often his family had moved before he was twelve years old. "The lack of a fixed address in Portland during that critical period in his early life," writes McBride, "no doubt helped instill in him the intense feelings about home and wandering that animate so much of his work."

As Ford returned to Monument Valley repeatedly after World War II, he would gradually dot its immensity with the symbols of family society: a church, a homestead, a school, a graveyard. As Kathleen Neils Conzen has noted, "Time and again, in memoirs and novels, folk songs and films, political speeches and academic histories, Americans have insisted that the story of Western settlement is a story of the conquest of nature and the taming of human nature in the name of the family and of the community that families together form."

In *My Darling Clementine* (1946), the image of Monument Valley is more austere. Now limned against lowering skies, buttes merely glimpsed from a distance in *Stagecoach* loom ominously over Wyatt Earp and his brothers. "Sure is rough-lookin' country," muses Wyatt, as he surveys a desert scrub far removed from the "sweet water up yonder" that he craves for his cattle. The town of Tombstone serves, ironically, as the fulcrum of life in *My Darling Clementine,* while the valley, a somber terrain in the monochrome cinematography of Ford's cameraman Joe MacDonald, endures as a privileged burial ground for young James Earp, with Merrick Butte and the Mittens watching over his grave.

Ford seeks the spirit of the Old West, at the ready expense of strict geographical or historical authenticity. The real Tombstone lies almost four hundred miles to the south of Monument Valley, near the Mexican border. When Wyatt Earp remarks that his brother Morg is "riding shot at Tucson," it sounds like a nearby cow town, but in fact Tucson is more than three hundred miles due south of Ford's location. These towns sprang up in southeastern Arizona—the notorious Arizona Territory that, during the 1880s, became a bloody hunting ground for Geronimo and his Apache warriors—as Americans moved westward, just as other settlements whose names resound with significance, such as Abilene, Wichita, and Dodge City, had arisen not long before and not all that far to the northeast. The fact that Newton Earp was the only one of the six actual Earp brothers to avoid trouble did not bother Ford, nor did *My Darling Clementine* make any reference to Wyatt's reputation as a horse thief and stagecoach robber as well as a sometime lawman. Perpetuating a distorted legend was, after all, a characteristic trait in the fiction of Bret Harte that Ford had grown up reading.

So Ford constructs his own mythical domain, underpinned by the tension between the frontier West and the flawed, irresolute East as embodied by Clementine and Doc Holliday. Not just the imagery but also the very locale is

Victor Mature and, in the background, Henry Fonda in *My Darling Clementine*. Ford's manipulation of perspective enhances a sense of distance between the two men.

romantic to a point that effaces the bitterness of Wyatt's discovery of his murdered brother in the rain. In an Anthony Mann Western, what one recalls is the abrasive dialogue and the bitter acceptance of loss. Ford refuses to comply with this way of the world, opting instead for a vision of life in the semi-wilderness that's purged of rancor. The three most conspicuous traits in the real Doc Holliday's personality—his drinking, his tubercular cough, and his controlled explosions of temper—have marked all the principal screen portraits of this perplexing character. But Ford was always willing to take liberties, on matters large or small. In surviving photographs, Doc sports a mustache; Victor Mature, however, does not.

Doc Holliday may have mislaid his self-respect in the smoke-hung bars of Tombstone and other towns (page 57), but Henry Fonda's Wyatt Earp seems to cherish the very air and space and horizons of this exalted land. As he emerges, reluctantly fragrant from the barber's shop, Wyatt surveys the town and the distant mesa, and all's right with his world. Ford's gift for distilling emotion could not be better expressed than in the sequence—almost a largo—when Wyatt Earp strolls with Clementine (Cathy Downs) from Tombstone's main set of buildings down to the incipient church site. Arm in arm, they walk past the barber's saloon ("Tonsorial Parlor") in the slow, portentous rhythm reserved for bridal couples negotiating the aisle. Offscreen, a distant congregation sings "Shall We Gather at the River."

Wyatt and Clem swing right, then move down onto the dusty street and head toward the congregation, with the spindly scaffolding of the church tower against the sky of Monument Valley. No further courtship seems necessary. They pause beneath the temporary wooden platform built for the church, and they watch as the locals dance in cheerful abandon to the strains of "Oh, Dem Golden Slippers." Wyatt must pluck courage from some half-forgotten protocol; he removes his hat and turns to Clem with a bashful "Would you oblige me, ma'am?" And when at last Russell Simpson's mustachioed deacon yells to the crowd to "make way for our new marshal and his lady fair," Wyatt Earp's final bastion of reluctance succumbs to the mood of the moment (opposite). The emotional commitment will take care of itself.

The dance scene in *My Darling Clementine,* filmed on the site of the present Visitors Center in Monument Valley

Ford had remembered Fonda's "jolting awkwardness in the square dance in *The Grapes of Wrath* and he resolved then and there to exploit the humanizing potential of Fonda's lurch-steps on every possible future occasion." As Wyatt and Clem dance to the infectious tune, their joy communicates itself to each and every one of the settlers. It embodies a ritual as timeless and as touching as any in the Native American vocabulary. It's the manifest reconciliation between two worlds that fascinates Ford here: the dusty, inarticulate cattleman and the prim, well-dressed lass from the East. As J. A. Place has noted, "Earp passes between the best values of East and West with no real problem, and he is the last Fordian hero to do so." The gigantic bauxite block of Mitchell Butte in the background of the valley stands like a symbolic altar for the ceremony. (The set for this scene was built on the site of the present Visitors Center at the northern entrance to Monument Valley.)

Ford, like Tchaikovsky, declares his pathos without shame. Callow young James Earp thinks he possesses a solid silver emblem, but it's merely brass. No matter. The pendant will pass from a cowardly Clanton to the gullible Chihuahua, who also finds its innocence untarnished. Doc Holliday's predicament is the most poignant aspect of the film: so much absorbed, so little learned. His reputation as a surgeon "back East," his cultivated voice, the nostalgic photograph of him on some college sports team, and especially his unexpected knowledge of Shakespeare all confirm that a life has somehow been diminished by exposure to the coarse-cut temptations of the West. Accustomed to running before the storm, the tubercular Doc jumps on a stagecoach bound for the Mexican border. When Wyatt catches up with him (near the North Window of Monument Valley), the traditional gunfight ends with Doc suffering a wounded hand—saved by the lenient marshal for a more significant gesture. Unlike the drunken doctor in *Stagecoach,* who redeems himself by delivering Mrs. Mallory's baby in extremis, John Holliday fails to save his mistress from her gunshot injury. He can find atonement only in death as, having killed one of the Clantons, he succumbs to his wounds behind a wooden fence during the shootout at the O.K. Corral, leaving his white handkerchief to flutter on the barrier—a symbol not just of surrender, but also of a tenderness extinguished.

The "Regulars"

John Ford, like Ingmar Bergman later, fostered a vivacious gallery of supporting players, from Ward Bond to Ben Johnson and from Victor McLaglen to Harry Carey Jr., among many others. His sentiment even extended to employing the Western stars of yesteryear, such as Tom Tyler in *She Wore a Yellow Ribbon,* Hoot Gibson in *The Horse Soldiers* (below), and most poignant of all, George O'Brien in *Cheyenne Autumn*—the same George O'Brien who, as Davy Brandon, had cast such a glamorous spell over *The Iron Horse* some forty years earlier.

Old comrades: Hoot Gibson and John Ford share a light while on location for *The Horse Soldiers*.

The first of Ford's regulars, Harry Carey Sr. (1878–1947), was a stalwart of his early career. Harry Dewitt Carey had starred in D. W. Griffith films such as *The Musketeers of Pig Alley* (1913) and then, drawn to the burgeoning Western genre, joined Universal in Hollywood in 1915. His first Western for Ford was a three-reeler entitled *The Soul Herder* (1917), a film that the director later considered as his true debut in motion pictures. He came of age for Ford with the ambivalent role of Cheyenne Harry in the feature-length *Straight Shooting* (also 1917), a powerful story of conflict between ranchers and cattlemen, with Carey playing the contract killer who responds to his troubled conscience when sent to kill a recalcitrant old farmer.

Carey made more than twenty Westerns with Ford over the next four years. His restrained performances suggest an immense well of self-assurance, and his unadorned good looks exude an offbeat glamour that persuaded audiences of the authenticity of the Westerns they were watching. When Ford turned to other genres, his relationship with Carey diminished, although nothing could destroy their mutual admiration. In the wake of Carey's death, Ford dedicated *3 Godfathers* (1948) to his memory, with a credit referring to him as a "Bright Star of the early Western sky." He also gave one of the main roles in that film to Carey's son, Harry Carey Jr., affectionately known as "Dobe."

The flame-haired Harry Carey Jr. (born 1921) remained close to Ford's heart, primarily because he was the son of Ford's first great star in the silent era. But he never acceded to leading parts. Instead, in numerous supporting roles (opposite, top), he contributed a blend of softness and good humor, flecked on occasion by an outburst of ill temper springing from exasperation at either losing the girl or resenting an officer.

Ben Johnson (1918–1996), so charismatic in *Rio Grande,* had a frank exchange of views with Ford during the shooting of *Wagon Master* and was banished from favor for almost fourteen years, until

Harry Carey Jr., known as "Dobe," in *She Wore a Yellow Ribbon*

Ford and two of his favorite actors, John Wayne and Ben Johnson, during the shooting of *She Wore a Yellow Ribbon*

Ward Bond as the Reverend Captain Sam Clayton (left), with John Wayne as Ethan Edwards, repelling an Indian attack in *The Searchers*

Ford cast him, uncredited, as a trooper in *Cheyenne Autumn*. As Sergeant Tyree in *She Wore a Yellow Ribbon,* Johnson (page 63, bottom) emerges as the most astute man in his troop, distinguishing the mark of a Southern Cheyenne dog soldier on an arrow and, later, "reading" the mind of a hot-blooded brave.

Ward Bond (1903–1960) remained at Ford's side for almost thirty years. Often a figure of fun, he had served a long apprenticeship in Westerns and B movies during the 1930s before Ford gave him the juicy part of John Palmer Cass in *Young Mr. Lincoln*. Bond's hectoring manner, reinforced by a prizefighter's physique, set him apart from most of the other actors in Ford's stable. He would yell and bluster his way through Westerns such as *My Darling Clementine, Fort*

Apache, and eventually *The Searchers* (opposite), in which, as the Bible-toting Texas Ranger with a stovepipe hat, he served as social foil to John Wayne's disillusioned Ethan Edwards. Bond's most engaging role was as the Mormon elder in *Wagon Master,* taking the name of the Lord in vain and then instantly apologizing. Bond's natural exuberance appealed to Ford—along with his ability to drink with the best of them off the set. Despite enjoying the charisma of a leader, Bond never had a starring role.

The reputation of Victor McLaglen (1883–1959) will survive more from Ford's later Westerns and Irish dramas than from his long-vanished stardom in the 1930s. Born in the sedate English town of Tunbridge Wells, McLaglen would accentuate his Irish brogue to great advantage. By the early 1920s he had starred in several British films, and in 1924 he went to Hollywood, where he played the lead in J. Stuart Blackton's Western *The Beloved Brute.* He won top billing in Ford's *Hangman's House* (1928) and *The Lost Patrol* (1934), before receiving an Academy Award for *The Informer* (1935). McLaglen's portrayal of Gypo Nolan, the dim-witted Irishman who cannot help betraying his pal and comrade-in-arms during the "struggles," recalls the best acting work of Emil Jannings, and visually the film owes much to German expressionism, Fritz Lang's *M* in particular.

During the next two decades, McLaglen reveled in a number of supporting roles for Ford—in the words of Joseph McBride, "as an Irish buffoon, broadly but delightfully played." Who can forget his leering sergeants in the cavalry trilogy: Festus Mulcahy in *Fort Apache* (page 66) and Timothy Quincannon in *She Wore a Yellow Ribbon* and *Rio Grande*. In these films, he embodies the rough-edged but good-as-gold spirit of the U.S. Army in Ford's vision of the post–Civil War West. Officious to his fingertips, he relishes the moment in *Rio Grande* when he instructs Ben Johnson and Harry Carey Jr. to ride

Sergeant Mulcahy (Victor McLaglen) tries the spiked punch in *Fort Apache* as (left to right) Sergeants Beaufort (Pedro Armendariz), Quincannon (Dick Foran—although McLaglen plays Sergeant Quincannon in *She Wore a Yellow Ribbon* and *Rio Grande*), and Shattuck (Jack Pennick, Ford's pal and bit player for more than thirty years) await their turns.

two horses at once, one foot on each saddle—like "the ancient Romans," he adds with a beam of pride. Addicted to the devil brew in *She Wore a Yellow Ribbon,* he's a Falstaff in waiting, rousing Captain Nathan Brittles (John Wayne) at dawn and taking a swig from a well-concealed whiskey bottle. "You've a breath on you like a hot mince pie," declares Brittles indulgently. Where Ward Bond's character usually takes himself very seriously, even pompously, McLaglen's can always laugh slyly at his own expense.

Ford had a knack of adjusting McLaglen's costumes to suit his temper—suspenders and sergeant's cap one moment, a hefty tweed suit the next. He bade unknowing farewell to his favorite Irish roustabout in *The Quiet Man,* when McLaglen plunged heart and soul into the character of Squire "Red" Will Danaher, older brother of fiery Mary Kate (Maureen O'Hara). Not for the first time in Ford's films, McLaglen swung his fists like mighty mallets, and for the last time he was obliged to scowl and accept defeat. After all, he was sixty-nine at the time.

Beyond his regulars, Ford could coax unforgettable performances from actors not known for their subtlety. Think of Lee Marvin (1924–1987), for example, who tackled the role of Liberty Valance with a sadistic, sneering relish that is so unpleasant it almost tickles one's sympathies. Marvin's sheer swaggering authority can flourish only because the fiber of Shinbone's leading citizens is as flaccid as the marshal's paunch. And how can one forget Victor Mature (1915–1999) as Doc Holliday in *My Darling Clementine,* who for once in his career suggests that he might actually know the words of Shakespeare's "To Be or Not to Be" soliloquy?

Ford admirers will note that some of the director's most familiar "regulars"—Thomas Mitchell, John Carradine, Andy Devine, and other favorites—feature only sporadically in his Westerns.

In *Wagon Master* (1950), Ford returns to an antebellum time and topic: the Mormon migration to their "promised land" in present-day Utah. Set in 1849, this low-budget Western runs for a mere eighty minutes but endures as one of Ford's most eccentric and lovable films. While shooting *She Wore a Yellow Ribbon* in Monument Valley one year earlier, Ford had been impressed by his Mormon extras—"their hardworking spirit and dancing skills, along with their devotion to a marginalized religious faith." Although he did not share their faith, Ford perceived

Albert Bierstadt. *A Surveyor's Wagon in the Rockies.* c. 1859. Oil on paper mounted on Masonite, 8 x 13⅛". The Saint Louis Art Museum. Gift of J. Lionberger Davis

Wagon Master: Ford uses the extended line of the wagon train to amplify and deepen his image.

in these migrants a genuine democratic spirit, and in casting Russell Simpson as Brother Perkins and Jane Darwell as the antic Sister Ledeyard, he evoked memories of these two actors in *The Grapes of Wrath,* with its similarly trundling journey into the West.

Joseph Smith had founded the Mormon Church in 1830, and he had established himself in Ohio and also in Missouri. But the authorities regarded the Mormons as a threat to the entrenched system of slavery and loathed their religious fanaticism. Smith was arrested and then murdered by a mob while being held in jail in Carthage, Illinois, in 1844. Under the leadership of Brigham Young (referred to as "Brother Young" in *Wagon Master*), the Mormons then trekked for more than a thousand miles westward to Utah. An advance party reached the Great Salt Lake in July 1847, and during the next two decades some eighty thousand Mormon pioneers managed to travel to Salt Lake City—and the opening of the transcontinental railroad accelerated the pace of the migration. In *The Oregon Trail*, published in 1849, Francis Parkman wrote: "After half an hour's riding, we saw the white wagons of the Mormons drawn up among the trees. Axes were sounding, trees were falling, and log-huts going up along the edge of the woods and upon the adjoining meadow. As we came up the Mormons left their work and seated themselves on the timber around us, when they began earnestly to discuss points of lamentation over the loss of their great temple of Nauvoo" (the town they had established in Illinois in 1839).

Ford makes his band of Mormons a microcosm of the whole westward migration. "Next summer," declares Ward Bond's Elder Wiggs, "there'll be a hundred families on the move, and they're countin' on us to have a crop ready for 'em." Much later, he talks with burning zeal of the importance of getting their sacks of grain across the San Juan River. Anthony Mann would similarly describe the homesteaders' need for plants and seeds in *Bend of the River,* made two years later. Ford also takes every opportunity to illustrate the Mormon fondness for music, with dancing on boards to traditional folk melodies, as well as an admittedly tentative group dance around the fire with some gentle Navajo.

Wagon Master, shot in Moab Valley, Utah, in Professor Valley, and around Fisher Towers and Locomotive Rock, contains some of the most ravishing imagery ever achieved by Ford in monochrome (page 69). By accentuating the length of the wagon train, Ford and his cameraman, Bert Glennon, gave a stereoscopic depth to the image. Wagons trundle wearily along desert trails, horses dip their heads to drink in the smooth waters of the San Juan, and everywhere the rising dust catches the light in a magical affirmation of the pioneering cause. The arduous physical experience of the pioneers is encapsulated in a single brilliant shot toward the end of the film, as more than a dozen wagons climb laterally across an escarpment— filmed long before digital matting would have created such an image in the lab. Despite this dreamy texture, *Wagon Master* was actually made pretty close to where the story unfolded. Costar Ben Johnson talks about "Navajo country, southwest of here," and the San Juan River and valley are very close to Moab.

She Wore a Yellow

relish by George Bancroft and Andy Devine respectively. He also introduced the theme of bourgeois hypocrisy, which Ford loathed throughout his life, and which makes villains of such "respectable" folk as Hatfield (John Carradine) and Gatewood.

The characters in *Stagecoach* offer a microcosm of the West as Ford envisioned it. It is a domain filled with the fugitive and the maverick. Mrs. Mallory exemplifies the well-educated and overly protected Easterner, at home in the military aristocracy and liable to faint at the first sign of savagery (and not just because she happens to be in a late stage of pregnancy). Dallas (Claire Trevor), the "fallen woman" with a heart of gold, typifies those who had stumbled beneath the wheels of a pioneering society that grasped its pleasures with neither thought nor feeling, while retaining the puritanical postures of yesteryear.

Ford knows how to display such contradictions in a humorous vein. The tipsy figure of Doc Boone appears first in a state of some confusion, pursued by his landlady and the arch and shrill reproaches of the Law and Order League. Quoting a couple of lines from Marlowe's *Tamburlaine,* he poaches one's sympathies without much effort, subliminally abetted by the strains of "Shall We Gather at the River" on the soundtrack. Ford would create similar roles for Alan Mowbray in *My Darling Clementine* and *Wagon Master,* and for Edmond O'Brien in *The Man Who Shot Liberty Valance,* hinting that a cultivated mind is worth more than any amount of propriety. It is almost, but not quite, a caricature of Western society and its personalities who either cling to the vestiges of respectability or, with a flourish, flout them.

Ford's films demonstrate that not all villains in the Old West were unshaven outlaws or bloodthirsty Apache. In *Stagecoach,* the two most odious characters are Gatewood, the banker who robs his own bank, and Hatfield, the Southern "gentleman" who glides to the protection of Mrs. Mallory. Gatewood, ultraconservative and humorless in the extreme, owns The Miners' and Cattlemen's Bank, implying that he plunders the two staple revenue earners of the American West. Carradine gives the gambler Hatfield an ominous twist similar to that of the infamous Caldwell, the role he created in *Drums Along the Mohawk* that same year.

Preparing to film an exterior shot in *Stagecoach,* starring John Wayne as the Ringo Kid (emerging from the conveyance)

The Western genre had nurtured many a dashing champion, from Harry Carey to Tom Mix. In John Wayne's Ringo Kid (page 79), however, Ford dares to present a hero more complex and diffident than his predecessors, a man whose past affects his conduct, and whose modesty exasperates men and entrances women. Introduced in a startling rush of a dolly shot, as if surging up from the desert, Ringo twirls his rifle and changes forever the career of both Wayne himself and Ford. The tenderness and vulnerability at the core of the Kid will become essential qualities in every Ford hero, whether played by John Wayne, Henry Fonda, James Stewart, or Richard Widmark. He is drawn not to the strong but to the weak; he is puzzled by pomposity, irked by chauvinism. Ford illustrates these traits well in a series of close-ups of Ringo hunkered down in the coach, glancing up to left and right at his traveling companions in response to their words and actions.

"The taming of human nature" indeed. Ford's Westerns are fraught with dangers more insidious than those presented by the desert wilderness. In *Stagecoach,* the arrogant banker Gatewood and the suave, gimlet-eyed Hatfield have learned how best to exploit the naïveté of many settlers and, even more, their tremulous visitors from the East.

The U.S. Cavalry occupies a minor role in the film, yet even here it shields the white settlers and visitors from Indian attack, following the stagecoach discreetly in the first part of the film, then riding to its rescue like a deus ex machina toward the end. Holt's cavalry officer prefigures more rounded portrayals of soldiers played by Ben Johnson, Harry Carey Jr., and Jeffrey Hunter in subsequent Ford Westerns (see also Chapter 5).

Stagecoach: The archetypal Ford image, with the full panoply of Monument Valley in the background (and snow lingering on the desert floor)

John Wayne

John Wayne (1907–1979) had appeared in small roles in three John Ford pictures—*Hangman's House* (1928), *Salute* (1929), and *Men Without Women* (1930)—but when his starring opportunity came, it was given to him not by Ford but by Raoul Walsh, in *The Big Trail* (1930). However, that Western bombed at the box office, and throughout the next decade Wayne labored in comparative obscurity. Unlike Gene Autry and Roy Rogers, Wayne could not sing—at least melodiously—and did not attract a wide following.

Ford knew, however, that Wayne was the perfect choice to play the Ringo Kid in *Stagecoach*. The two men had remained fast friends during the 1930s, and Ford offered him a part that not even Gary Cooper could have filled to such perfection. When, after more than a quarter hour of screen time, the stagecoach pulls up at the sound of a single shot, and Bert Glennon's camera dollies hastily toward the figure of John Wayne, it's as though a myth had walked out of a door, as Dilys Powell once wrote of Orson Welles. Twirling his rifle with his right hand and clutching his saddle and cloth with the other, he stands tall against the backdrop of mesa and buttes. Wayne may not have been as muscular as George O'Brien, or as rugged as Victor McLaglen, but on the screen he moves with a lissome grace, and the vulnerable kindness in his eyes gives him an appealing quality denied to monolithic heroes of the sagebrush (opposite).

The Ringo Kid has relatively few lines to play with, but as a cowboy he's condemned to social exile with that quintessence of sin, Claire Trevor's Dallas. He reserves his most dazzling smile for Dallas, preferring her unabashed candor to the dainty, reserved, and fragile mien of Mrs. Mallory. Wayne's gentility under the circumstances

John Wayne off the set during the making of *Stagecoach*. Portrait by Ned Scott. © 1978 Ned Scott Archive/MPTV.net

makes the other men appear boorish and insensitive. When, smitten by Dallas, he follows her out through a lighted doorway, he does so with the same kindling hope as Martha Edwards in the opening shot of *The Searchers*.

Ford contrasts this introspective aspect of the Kid with the deftness of his traditional Western skills—kneeling on the roof of the fleeing coach, picking off Indians with unerring aim, leaping from horse to galloping horse in order to keep the team in harness (although Yakima Canutt actually performed this latter stunt). Wayne's laconic line to Dallas, "We ain't never gonna say good-bye," rings like a refrain for all the years to come with Ford. Wayne would appear in *The Long Voyage Home, They Were Expendable, Fort Apache, 3 Godfathers, She Wore a Yellow Ribbon, Rio Grande, The Quiet Man, The Searchers, The Wings of Eagles, The Horse Soldiers, The Man Who Shot Liberty Valance, How the West Was Won,* and *Donovan's Reef*—thirteen more films, with eight Westerns or partial Westerns among them.

In *Fort Apache,* Wayne must play second fiddle to Henry Fonda's misguided zealot of a colonel. Once a regimental commander himself, he is reduced to a mere echo of his officious superior. Colonel Thursday contradicts even the most minor order that York issues, overruling him with peremptory decrees.

One identifies with Captain Kirby York, however, notably at the climax when he tries to rescue a wounded Thursday and forestall a massacre. So often accused of stolidity, a softer Wayne in this scene communicates much through looks and stance; feelings of anger, regret, and grudging admiration seem to flicker behind his officer's gaze. He plays the same character in *Rio Grande,* but now he has become at once more important—commanding officer at Fort Starke, no less—and more intractable. Haughty toward both his son and his estranged wife, Lieutenant Colonel Kirby York requires the adrenaline

John Wayne in his most poignant role for Ford: Nathan Brittles in *She Wore a Yellow Ribbon*

charge of heroism to chasten him. His mustache and tiny beard (mere fuzz in his dimpled chin) give Wayne a look of severity that's dispelled only when he tells his wife, "I never want to kiss you good-bye, Kathleen"—an echo of those words to Dallas near the end of *Stagecoach*. Wounded by an Apache arrow, he tells his son to pull it out. And when he sinks back after the deed is done, it's as though the venom of his prejudice against his former life has been extracted.

In Nathan Brittles, Wayne found his most sentimental yet most rewarding role for John Ford (below). *She Wore a Yellow Ribbon* may discomfort critics with its tendency toward tears, but Brittles, a cavalry veteran on the verge of retirement, exemplifies the soft fist beneath the iron glove of Ford's brusque nature. Like his Cheyenne counterpart, Pony That Walks (Chief John Big Tree), Brittles is obliged to cede power to the next generation. Both men regard with

dismay the choleric, impetuous leanings of the younger men around them. Like some aging detective pleading for just one more chance to crack a case, Brittles wants to venture out into the desert in a final sortie to save the life of Lieutenant Flint Cohill (John Agar). He reveals his sensitivity on various occasions, not least when, moved by a wounded corporal's pain, he agrees to the doctor's plea that the troop dismount and proceed at marching pace. Wayne is at his relaxed best in his bantering moments with Victor McLaglen's whiskey-breathed sergeant. Their repartee mitigates the sentimentality to which Ford succumbs in scenes such as the final review of the troop, where Lieutenant Pennell (Harry Carey Jr.) presents Brittles with a silver watch, engraved with the words "Lest We Forget."

When Brittles does retire, he has nowhere to go but toward the western horizon. He exemplifies the professional soldier whose entire career has been devoted to extending and protecting the frontier dividing whites from Indians, civilization from barbarity, East from West. Yet, like James Stewart in Delmer Daves's *Broken Arrow* (1950), Wayne in *She Wore a Yellow Ribbon* has earned the respect of Native Americans. As he enters the enemy encampment to parley with Pony That Walks, a furious young brave fires an arrow into the sand at his feet. Wayne picks it up, snaps it deliberately in two, spits on the pieces, and then flings them back in the face of the horseman. The gestures, the timing, are paramount. A less sensitive, less courageous soldier would be cut to pieces within seconds.

Wayne thought *The Searchers* to be "the best picture Ford ever made," and his role as Ethan Edwards was certainly the most courageous the actor accepted until 1976, when he agreed to play John Books in Don Siegel's *The Shootist,* a man dying of cancer—like Wayne himself. Ethan's bitterness drags at him like an anchor—he still chafes at the Confederacy's defeat in the Civil War three years earlier;

Ethan Edwards (John Wayne) prepares to follow a solitary destiny in the closing shot of *The Searchers*. Ford's use of the doorway neatly refers to the opening shot of the film—although the cabin and the landscape are different.

he has coveted his brother's wife so long that, like the dead Comanche warrior whose eyes he fires at, he must "wander forever between the winds"; and her murder only enflames a long-smoldering hatred of the Indian race. In short, Ethan must be the most unsympathetic "hero" in all of Ford's work.

The contradictions in Wayne's persona are more manifest in *The Searchers* than in any other Ford Western. Jean-Luc Godard asked himself how he could "hate John Wayne upholding Goldwater and yet love him tenderly when abruptly he takes Natalie Wood into his arms in the last reel of *The Searchers*."

Yet the sheer tarnished humanity of the man makes one warm to him. One enjoys his sparring with Ward Bond's pompous, blustering, unholy blend of reverend and Texas Ranger. One exonerates him for the justified homicide of Jerem Futterman (Peter Mamakos), another of those repellent traders who live like carrion off the conflict between Indians and white men. One admires him, finally, for his ability to jump beyond his own shadow and spare Debbie—who is both his niece and a longtime captive of the Indians—from his wrath. Ford leaves him to fret with his conscience in the searing sun as he delivers Debbie to the Jorgensens' home and then turns away toward his solitude (page 87), clutching his right arm with his left in a gesture so beloved of Harry Carey Sr., Ford's first Western star. One's thoughts go not with any of the other characters but with Wayne's, as the door of the house shuts implacably on his tall, chastened figure.

In both *The Horse Soldiers* and Ford's episode in *How the West Was Won,* Wayne plays senior soldiers who have become efficient and dispassionate with their advancing years, hiding their emotions beneath a carapace of experience. As Colonel Marlowe in the earlier film (opposite), Wayne takes his orders from General William Tecumseh Sherman, while in the later one he himself incarnates the general. Gruff and obdurate, Colonel Marlowe nurses a bitterness similar to that of Ethan Edwards, comprising a loathing of Indians and resentment toward any member of the medical profession, in the wake of his wife's dying during a botched operation. Ford undermines Marlowe's rancor by introducing the poignant music ("Debbie's Theme") from *The Searchers* in scenes such as Marlowe's adieu to the Southern belle (Constance Towers). This time, however, he belongs to the Union Army. Whether wearing the blue of the North or the washed-out, terra-cotta red of the South, Wayne exemplifies Ford's vision of him as a soldier per se.

Wayne gives his most discreet of all performances for Ford in *The Man Who Shot Liberty Valance*. He takes top billing ahead of James Stewart, but his character, Tom Doniphon, resents the limelight. He rides unobtrusively into town in dead of night, bringing in the injured

The Horse Soldiers: John Wayne in a heroic stance above the Mississippi River

Ransom Stoddard (Stewart), who has suffered a beating at the hands of Liberty Valance. Tom may be the deus ex machina who saves Stoddard in the climactic gunfight with Valance, yet in so doing he loses the woman he loves, for Hallie (Vera Miles) will now revere not him but Stoddard. The latter is, after all, a lawyer who can teach her to read and write, who brings a whiff of civilization from the distant East Coast. These are skills that lie beyond the grasp of Doniphon, who may be the most poignant personality ever created on screen by Wayne, on a par with his role in *The Shootist*. This quiet-spoken man, so supremely confident in his own sharpshooting ability, lacks in love the sort of killer instinct he extols to all and sundry throughout the movie. Ford, one feels, favors Wayne. If only, he seems to be saying, all

Ford demonstrates how John Wayne should receive one of many blows, during the filming of *The Horse Soldiers*.

OVERLAND STAGE LINE & DEPOT.

John Ford on location for *The Man Who Shot Liberty Valance,* with two of his most trusted actors in later years, James Stewart and John Wayne

Westerners would manifest Doniphon's self-effacing strength and acceptance of things as they are. As civilization gradually comes to Shinbone and similar Western townships, Doniphon's character seems destined, like old soldiers, not to die but just to fade away.

The bitterness that flowed from the surrender at Gettysburg adds to the friction between Lieutenant Colonel Owen Thursday and his subordinates in *Fort Apache* (1948). Thursday despises an "ex-reb" like Sergeant Beaufort (Pedro Armendariz), even if he recognizes the man's ability to speak Spanish and thus help in negotiating with Cochise. Thursday damns General Robert E. Lee with faint praise when he mentions a paper that Lee wrote during his time at West Point, making arcane reference to the maneuver deployed by Genghis Khan at the Battle of Kin-Sha in 1221.

The author behind Ford's cavalry trilogy, James Warner Bellah, sympathized with the Confederacy and wallowed in imperialist lore, quoting Rudyard Kipling's definition of empire as "the white man's burden." Ford had the shrewdness of vision to call on Frank S. Nugent, then film critic of the *New York Times,* to help soften the harsh outlines of Bellah's fiction. Nugent introduced the female characters into the first two films, as well as much of the banter. These sturdy, resilient women would people Ford's Westerns and historical movies through *The Horse Soldiers,* helping to keep the macho officers on their toes and to point up their often absurd arrogance and pomposity.

Ford's two most controversial Westerns happen to be those dealing with specific events in history: *Fort Apache* and *Cheyenne Autumn.* Nugent based his screenplay for *Fort Apache* on a Bellah story entitled "Massacre," which in turn stemmed from "Bugles in the Afternoon" by Ernest Haycox, the author of the story that became *Stagecoach.* The American cinema has frequently been drawn to the graphic intensity of George Armstrong Custer (opposite) and his defeat at the Little Big Horn in Montana on June 25, 1876. Thomas Ince's *Custer's Last Fight* dates from 1912, Raoul Walsh's *They Died with Their Boots On* from 1941, Roy Rowland's *Bugles in the Afternoon* from 1952, Robert Siodmak's *Custer of the West* (featuring Robert Shaw as Custer) from 1967, and of course Arthur Penn's *Little Big Man,* with Dustin Hoffman's character startled to find himself on the battlefield next to a deranged Custer, from 1970. Ford and his screenwriter deliberately chose to blur the precise comparisons with Custer's demise. The film unfolds in Arizona, not in Montana. The original short story's Fort Starke has become Fort Apache, and the Apache themselves have replaced the Sioux.

Charles C. Schreyvogel.
Custer's Demand.
1903. Oil on canvas,
54 x 79". From the
Collection of the
Gilcrease Museum,
Tulsa, Oklahoma

Charles C. Schreyvogel.
Attack at Dawn.
1904. Oil on canvas,
34 x 46". From the
Collection of the
Gilcrease Museum,
Tulsa, Oklahoma

Fort Apache: Ford
always sought to cap-
ture the energy and
drama of the West.

If the massacre at the Little Big Horn extinguished one long-held myth—that of the invincible white soldier routing the savage Indians—then it gave birth to another: that of the gallant, God-fearing officer who "died with his boots on" (in the film, Colonel Thursday) and whose bravery only underlines the need for further military action to ensure America's Manifest Destiny. *Fort Apache* refuses to endorse that myth, however, nowhere more so than in the final reel, in which the Western's staple ingredient, the "last-minute rescue," fails to appear. Ford also uses John Wayne's Captain York in a clever, calculating way. York becomes our alter ego in this absurd campaign against Cochise (who replaces Custer's nemesis Sitting Bull for the sake of convenience). York's is the voice of sweet reason in the confrontations with the Apache. He is the valiant subordinate officer who gallops into the canyon to try to rescue his benighted colonel.

Colonel Thursday in *Fort Apache* appears to be the most obdurate of all Ford's military officers. A martinet, utterly lacking in humor, he harbors a profound racial loathing of the Native American. He does concede some respect for the Sioux and the Cheyenne, but none for the Apache. The parallels with Custer are palpable, and they become unmistakable at the climax to the film, as Thursday leads his men on a doomed charge into an Indian ambush (opposite; filmed at Rock Door Canyon in Monument Valley, just behind Goulding's Lodge). Ironically, after his death, Thursday is exonerated in the eyes of visiting journalists by none other than Captain York, who enshrines him as a great soldier and maintains that the mythicized painting now hanging in Washington of Thursday's (read Custer's) last charge is "correct in every detail." Kirby then delivers a ringing encomium of the U.S. "regular army" and its men. They gaze with respect at Thursday's portrait as it hangs on a wall at the regimental headquarters, its frozen features contriving to perpetuate the illusion of virtue. In a final twist, York strides out wearing the outlandish headdress affected by Thursday (an equivalent to the dress gloves so beloved of Custer).

In *Fort Apache,* Ford promulgates for the first time his vision of everyday life in the frontier outposts, including rituals such as reveille and the raising of the flag

Misplaced heroism: The bugler prepares to sound the charge in *Fort Apache*.

(opposite), officers' call, and the training of recruits. Ford's fort is a place where relaxed soldiers sing dreamy serenades to beautifully dressed young women, and where formal dances and receptions are the order of the day. Cheerful army wives give furniture to a newcomer, and they maintain a stiff upper lip when their menfolk march off to battle. When a transfer arrives for Captain Collingwood (George O'Brien) just as he is departing to fight Cochise, his wife (Anna Lee) refuses to call him back. Instead she watches anxiously from the fort veranda. "I can't see him; all I can see is the flags," she murmurs poignantly. A vein of sentimentality always runs just beneath the surface of Ford's work; in *Fort Apache,* a tearful Sergeant Major O'Rourke (Ward Bond) is reunited with his son, to the strains of "Home Sweet Home," and the young lovers (John Agar and Shirley Temple) dance to the tune of "Goodnight Ladies" on the veranda, as a dance night comes to a close.

To be a soldier was to belong to a tightly knit family unit. Social divisions may have been evident, but when Thursday haughtily asserts that the class barrier cannot be breached, his sergeant major (Ward Bond) has the temerity to respond, "The army is not the whole world." The Irish sergeants in *Fort Apache,* akin to the trio in *The Iron Horse,* relish every opportunity of ridiculing the straitlaced pomposity of army customs. More seriously, these well-equipped aristocrats of the American military were not flameproof. Ford admitted, "The cavalry weren't all-American boys, you know. They made a lot of mistakes. . . . Custer, that was a pretty silly goddam expedition." For Ford, the abiding frivolity of the men in the ranks in fact undermined the rigid discipline required of troops along the frontier, even if it also serves in the films to stress their common humanity—for example, when Victor McLaglen's Sergeant Mulcahy and his pals get plastered on the "rotgut whiskey" concealed in the trader's storeroom. Ford nurses, one feels, a grudging admiration for Colonel Thursday's obsessive attention to dress. "The uniform, gentlemen, is not a subject for individual, whimsical expression," he tells his officers. "We're not cowboys at this post, or freighters with a load of alfalfa."

The flag is raised like a talisman against the dangers of the desert. This shot was filmed, for *She Wore a Yellow Ribbon,* from Goulding's Lodge at the northern entrance to Monument Valley.

Women in Ford's Westerns

Just as John Ford's cavalrymen are divided into raw recruits and seasoned officers, his female characters are either a fragile, protected species or sturdy pioneer women who have learned how to cope with the exigencies of life on the frontier. Claudette Colbert's Magdalena in *Drums Along the Mohawk* exemplifies the first type of heroine—tremulous, easily shocked, and loyal to her partner. In *Stagecoach,* the stark contrast between the delicate disdain of Louise Platt's Mrs. Mallory and the plainspoken, instinctive decency of Claire Trevor's Dallas becomes the fulcrum of the entire film. The relationship is summed up toward the end, when Mrs. Mallory, still weak after giving birth, turns to Dallas and murmurs, "If there's ever anything I can do for you. . . ." Dallas, recognizing the condescension but also the fact that Lucy Mallory is a prisoner of her class, replies, "I know . . ." (opposite).

In *My Darling Clementine,* Cathy Downs's Clementine Carter stands at a similar remove from Linda Darnell's Chihuahua, although here Ford's sympathies are more evenly divided. Clementine has none of the latent snootiness of Mrs. Mallory, while Chihuahua is altogether more provocative and maladroit than Dallas in *Stagecoach*. While Mrs. Mallory must undergo the trauma of childbirth, in *My Darling Clementine* it's the "fallen woman," Chihuahua, who undergoes an operation for a gunshot wound—but this time Doc Holliday's hand proves less sure than that of Doc Boone in the earlier film. So Ford rings the changes, from film to film.

In *Fort Apache,* Philadelphia Thursday (an unlikely name even for a patrician Easterner) gains much from the gusto of Shirley Temple's performance. She may wear a bonnet from Boston, and her father may be a domineering martinet, but Philadelphia flirts with the young officers of her fancy, and once fixed on Lieutenant Michael O'Rourke (John Agar, her husband in real life), she will not be set aside even by the colonel. Ford introduces various women "of a certain age" to serve as foils to Miss Thursday. Wives of veteran officers, they have buckled down to life at the fort and are eager to help a newcomer in their midst. They have become inured to the risk and folly of their husbands' occupation and the need to uphold a sense of honor, no matter what the consequences. Mrs. Collingwood in particular must cope with the realization that she could have saved her husband from certain death had she only run after the departing regiment and told him that his transfer had arrived.

Claire Trevor as Dallas in *Stagecoach,* clutching Mrs. Mallory's newborn baby

Joanne Dru's pert insouciance lit up Ford's West for a brief spell in the late 1940s. In *She Wore a Yellow Ribbon* as Olivia Dandridge (above), she wrings the heartstrings of two callow young officers and basks in the admiration of the aging Captain Brittles, for whom she summons up memories of his wife. Again, Ford includes an older woman in the narrative: Mildred Natwick's Abby Allshard, who deserves the sobriquet "Old Iron Pants" and rides out fearlessly with the soldiers when the going gets rough.

John Agar as the rather maladroit Lieutenant Cohill, and Joanne Dru as the "unspoilt" Easterner, in *She Wore a Yellow Ribbon*

Dru's part in *Wagon Master* suggests elements of the "fallen woman," but unlike Dallas in *Stagecoach* she wears her reputation with a salacious smile, getting Ben Johnson's Travis Blue in her sights. The Old West may have been the ideal romantic location in which love could blossom, but as *Wagon Master* illustrates, it could also be the hardest place for such sentiments to find fulfillment. One blink, and a woman could find herself a slave to drink as well as a "husband," like Fleuretty (Ruth Clifford), who staggers alongside Alan Mowbray's bogus quack, Dr. Hall, like a refugee from some minor Shakespearean comedy. Jane Darwell's Sister Ledeyard in the same film, lifting her horn to signal each new departure of the wagon train, epitomizes the durable spirit of the frontier family, a satiric riff on Darwell's role in *The Grapes of Wrath* (which, after all, was a Western with trucks in place of wagons).

As Ford grew older, so did his acknowledgment of the role played by such mature women. In both *The Searchers* and *Two Rode Together,* Olive Carey—the widow of Harry Carey Sr. and by then in her sixties—plays characters who communicate the no-nonsense pioneer spirit so appreciated by Ford. In *The Searchers,* she is an older version of Laurie Jorgensen (Vera Miles), whose fiery temperament eventually wins the heart and hand of Martin Pawley, played by Jeffrey Hunter (page 104).

Some of the most amusing moments in Ford's Western oeuvre involve women such as Laurie, as well as Hannah Hunter (Constance Towers) of *The Horse Soldiers*. They compete with men on equal terms, using not just feminine charm but also physical ingenuity, as when Hannah escapes her minders and almost betrays the Yankee presence to the Confederates across the river. Indeed, Hannah develops into a neat Southern equivalent of the familiar Eastern "lady" in Ford's Arizona-based Westerns. Genteel yet courageous, Hannah is

every bit as self-sufficient as Mary Beecher, the character Towers plays in *Sergeant Rutledge*. Mary may be introduced as the purported victim of some unmentionable crime at the hands of the black sergeant, but her demure comportment does not prevent her from shooting an Apache, then sitting all night with a rifle across her knees for fear of both the Indians and, if the official account that unfolds is to be believed, Sergeant Rutledge himself.

The shy lover confronted by the feisty female: Jeffrey Hunter and Vera Miles in *The Searchers*

Occasionally, Ford's condescending attitude toward women could brim to the surface. In *Two Rode Together,* Shirley Jones's Marty Purcell is treated by James Stewart's marshal with the same scorn and distaste that he metes out to white "squaw" captives. Hopelessly drunk, he almost delights in telling her that her missing brother will by now have grown up into a repellent Comanche "buck," reveling in the slaughter of whites.

Ford's personality could, however, also accommodate women who were altogether less easily intimidated—none better than Maureen O'Hara's Kathleen in *Rio Grande.* She emerges from the past of the seemingly impregnable Colonel York (John Wayne), to remind him that their marriage foundered in the wake of the Civil War. York had led his Yankee troops on an orgy of burning and looting, destroying his wife's Southern estate. Their only son, now serving with York's regiment, helps to bring the old partners together. O'Hara invests the part with dignity and a banked fury that at first baffles Kathleen's estranged husband, but finally convinces him that life together is better than life alone.

Perhaps the most rounded female character in Ford's later Western career is Vera Miles's Hallie Stoddard in *The Man Who Shot Liberty Valance.* For once, Ford shows a woman in both her prime and her senior years. Hallie exhibits the virtues of a pioneer female, running the family restaurant in Shinbone with the passionate efficiency of a Mildred Pierce, all the while responding to the compliments of Tom Doniphon (John Wayne) and Ransom Stoddard (James Stewart). Like the cactus rose she so admires, Hallie flourishes in inhospitable soil. Even though she's tricked by circumstance into believing Stoddard to be a hero, she soldiers on in her role as dutiful—and well-maintained—wife to the very end. Her heart may remain with the long-dead Doniphon, but her companion into old age will be Stoddard.

She Wore a Yellow Ribbon (1949), the second film in Ford's "cavalry trilogy," opens in the wake of Custer's defeat, with the Cheyenne now on the warpath. Sioux leaders Sitting Bull and Crazy Horse have united many tribes against the U.S. Cavalry. Captain Nathan Brittles (John Wayne) is on the verge of retirement, and the film revels in nostalgia for a pre-Custer era. Veterans of the Little Big Horn campaign are few and far between. Most of the troopers under Brittles's command are young and romantic, more interested in pursuing the immaculate Miss Dandridge (Joanne Dru) than they are the Indians (below). Throughout the cavalry trilogy, there's a pronounced contrast between the older, seasoned officers and the rough-edged recruits who have to be knocked into shape by the likes of Victor McLaglen's Sergeant Quincannon.

The fragility of the cavalry's hold over the territory (opposite) may be seen time and again in shots where the military columns are almost lost in the immensity of

The formal dance evening features in John Ford's cavalry pictures, including *She Wore a Yellow Ribbon*. From left to right: Harry Carey Jr., Joanne Dru, John Agar, John Wayne, Victor McLaglen, Mildred Natwick, and George O'Brien.

Nathan Brittles surveys
the Big Chief (a.k.a. Big
Indian) monument in
*She Wore a Yellow
Ribbon*.

the valley. Meanwhile, the Cheyenne—like other tribes in other Ford Westerns—dominate the landscape from the heights, echoing the archetypal composition as expressed by Francis Parkman: "High up on the top of the tallest bluff, conspicuous in the bright evening sunlight, sat a naked warrior on horseback, looking around, as it seemed, over the neighboring country." Yet there is also the image of a single rider, waving a signal against the skyline at dusk or dawn, which not only evokes the paintings of Frederic Remington but also signifies the defiance of the military.

Remington's *The Riderless Horse* (opposite) depicts a cavalry trooper galloping in some confusion, and to judge from the rifle that hangs from the mount beside him, he has lost a fellow soldier in some engagement. By almost suspending the horses in an ethereal space, Remington underlines the fear and lack of orientation of the cavalryman. In the film, the death of Private Smith, known affectionately as "Trooper," also illustrates this fortitude. Smith uses his final breath to commend young Sergeant Tyree to an attentive Captain Brittles. The captain pays tribute to the private because he knew Smith as nothing less than a brigadier general in the Confederacy.

The passing of the torch from one generation to another underscores Ford's military pictures. Brittles may at first fear for the future of his troop after his retirement, but by the close of the film he has recognized the courage and intelligence of young Tyree, as well as of Lieutenant Cohill, Brittles's successor. And the Civil War is invoked once again during the very last exchange of the film. Tyree, having raced after Brittles to hand him the news of his appointment as chief of scouts, says that the only endorsement missing is Robert E. Lee's. "Wouldn't have been bad," smiles the new lieutenant colonel, and the memory of the Confederacy lingers in the twilight. Wayne himself felt that Captain Brittles should have slipped away into the obscurity of the setting sun and "the new settlements in California," instead of being elevated to almost mythical proportions by his promotion and then sentimentalized in a finale back at Fort Starke (based on Fort Clark, in southwestern Texas).

Frederic Remington.
The Riderless Horse.
1886. Pencil, pen and
ink, and watercolor on
paper, 7⅞ x 11⅞".
Courtesy Sid Richard-
son Collection of
Western Art, Fort
Worth, Texas

The unhealed scars of the Civil War throb at the heart of *Rio Grande,* the final film in Ford's cavalry trilogy. Wayne again plays Kirby York (opposite), a troop captain in *Fort Apache* who is manifestly promoted to colonel in the final sequence. In *Rio Grande,* however, he is troubled not by his traumatic experiences in the shadow of the obsessed Owen Thursday, but by memories of the Civil War. As a Union Army officer under orders from General Philip Sheridan (J. Carroll Naish), he had plundered the South—in particular, his wife's plantation (an outrage that also had befallen the ancestors of Ford's wife, Mary, in South Carolina). Estranged ever since from her and from their son, Jeff (Claude Jarman Jr.), York is startled after fifteen years to discover that the boy has grown into a young man eager to join his regiment. Although much of the film's focus concerns the army's uncompromising pursuit of the Indians, the allusions to the Civil War underline once again the need for accommodation. Maureen O'Hara's Irish belle, Kathleen, stands for a South still feisty in the long aftermath of defeat, while the warm relationship between York and his superior, General Sheridan, stems from shared memories of the Shenandoah campaign of May 1864 (which includes the atrocities committed as part of it). In a subordinate theme, Tyree falls afoul of the authorities because he killed a Yankee down in Texas after being taunted about his sister. So the wounds still rankle.

Rio Grande becomes an essay in resignation, with York's life essentially saved by his son in the thick of battle. Jeff draws the Apache arrow from his father's shoulder, purging him symbolically—much as Martin will cleanse Ethan of another arrow's poison in *The Searchers.* Hauled back to Fort Starke on a dray, stripped of his uniform jacket, the colonel murmurs to his wife, "Our boy did well." Unity has been achieved, the kind of reconciliation that Ford imagines lay within the country's grasp in the early 1880s. In a postlude, the army band strikes up that most familiar of Southern marching songs, "Dixie," enabling Kathleen York to smile in acceptance of Sheridan's unspoken apology.

As J. A. Place has remarked of the military pictures, "the need to bend one's individual will to the military necessity becomes harder and harder to bear and finally, with *The Horse Soldiers* and then *Two Rode Together,* becomes of less value than individual priorities."

Rio Grande: The accoutrements of battle—Kirby York (John Wayne) with saber drawn, and the bugler about to sound the charge

Ford's pride in the cavalry reached a peak in one of his most underrated films, *The Horse Soldiers* (1959). John Wayne plays Colonel John Marlowe. He meets General William Tecumseh Sherman outside Vicksburg, Mississippi, which the North is desperate to take in 1863. The general says Newton Station must be destroyed, for it has been supplying the Confederate forces at Vicksburg. (The film drew its inspiration from the story of one Colonel Benjamin H. Grierson, who took seventeen hundred troopers with him deep into rebel territory during the spring of 1863, causing mayhem before they safely reached Union-held Baton Rouge, Louisiana.) Wayne's cantankerous colonel finds himself saddled with William Holden's Major Kendall, a surgeon assigned to Marlowe's regiment from General Ulysses S. Grant's headquarters.

The film encompasses two fundamental elements in Ford: the military man, for whom duty to the army precedes all else, and the ingrained humanism of the civilian doctor. (Doctors—invariably humorous—pop up all over Ford's Westerns, from Thomas Mitchell's inebriated Josiah Boone in *Stagecoach* to Guy Kibbee's Doc Wilkens in *Fort Apache,* from Victor Mature's Doc Holliday in *My Darling Clementine* to Chill Wills's Doc Wilkins in *Rio Grande*.) As the mission grows more hazardous, so Marlowe's abrasive manner reveals shades of unexpected subtlety. He spends time with a couple of deserters, acquiring information about Southern troop movements before knocking them both out. Once Newton Station has been overrun, Marlowe recoils in the face of his officers' gloating, and he finds himself moved by a young Yankee trooper who begs him to write to the youth's mother, before expiring in the doctor's arms. Like the Wayne characters in *Rio Grande* and *The Searchers,* Marlowe has an anguished past: two doctors operated in error on his wife, and her death has made him forever wary of the medical profession—which explains his attitude toward Kendall. He softens in the presence of Hannah Hunter (Constance Towers), the elegant Southern woman taken captive by the Northerners, and Ford brings up the plaintive musical theme ("Lorena") from *The Searchers* in the moments of their parting (opposite).

Even more poignant than the slaughter at Newton Station, a sequence showing youngsters entering battle is among Ford's finest achievements (page 114). To the

John Wayne and Constance Towers in *The Horse Soldiers*

The Horse Soldiers:
The cadets from
Jefferson Military
College are enlisted
by the Confederacy in
an attempt to stave
off the Union attack.

The Horse Soldiers:
The Union troops are
thrown into retreat by
the "boys' brigade"
from Jefferson Military
College.

Ford directs John Wayne and William Holden in *The Horse Soldiers*.

rousing sound of the drum and the fife, a battalion of cadets marches off from Jefferson Military College. One young cadet is dragged away by his distraught mother, an incident played for laughs by Ford, who always knows when to temper his tragic moments with a touch of levity. These raw recruits confront the startled Union cavalry, who retreat from the prospect of killing mere children (page 115). This time the music contributes a sardonic note new in Ford's attitude to the army.

Ford's heart may lie with the U.S. Cavalry, but he shares with Marlowe an instinctive dislike for bloodletting; he knows that the looting and wanton savagery exhibited by the Union forces at Newton Station are no better than many an Indian outrage committed in other Westerns. The tragedy of the Civil War lay in the confrontation between the ruthless efficiency of the North and the hotheaded, chaotic courage of the South, much as the nerveless English regiments of the eighteenth century had routed their impulsive Scottish foes.

Ford's conception of the antebellum South may be composed of belles, blacks, and ragamuffin hicks, but he cherished a nagging affection for the Confederacy, and many of his films' most intriguing characters have worn its colors, from Nathan Brittles in *She Wore a Yellow Ribbon* to Ethan Edwards in *The Searchers*.

Ford's segment of *How the West Was Won* lasts but twenty-two minutes. A monody for the loss of innocence in the Civil War, it carefully evades the temptation to see the struggle in mythical terms. Identifying with a perplexed country boy from Ohio, George Peppard's Zeb (page 118), Ford brings home the fear that transfixed first-time soldiers in the war. He re-creates the gruesome aftermath of the Battle of Shiloh, on April 6, 1862, in which James Stewart's Linus Rawlings (Zeb's father) dies, heaved off a bloody wooden bench in a makeshift hospital within, suitably, a church. "After Shiloh," intones Spencer Tracy's rasping voice offscreen, "the South never smiled."

In a moving vignette, Generals Grant (Harry Morgan) and Sherman (John Wayne) talk in the firelight after the battle (page 119). Grant seems ready to resign, convinced that he had ill prepared his troops for the Confederate attack. Some yards away, the exhausted Zeb has struck up a conversation with another soldier, who turns out to be a Southern deserter. When the "reb" recognizes Grant and raises his gun to assassinate him, Zeb has to restrain and finally bayonet his new-found friend to death. "Why did you make me *do* that?" he cries in frustration. It's a poignant rite of passage, filmed with discretion.

Death pursues the chastened Zeb even to his homecoming, where he finds the gravestones of his mother as well as his father in the garden beside their family cabin. Ford uses that most infectious of all Yankee battle songs, "When Johnny Comes Marching Home!" with stinging irony in this all too brief snapshot of the Civil War.

OPPOSITE
John Wayne as General William Tecumseh Sherman and Harry Morgan as General Ulysses S. Grant in Ford's Civil War episode of *How the West Was Won*.

Zeb Rawlings (George Peppard) bids farewell to his mother (Debbie Reynolds) in Ford's Civil War episode of *How the West Was Won*.

The cavalry at the charge—in *Stagecoach*, although it could just as easily be in three or four other Ford Westerns. The cavalry presented a fearsome image to the Native American.

CHAPTER 4

FORD AND THE NATIVE AMERICAN

"The heart of the Western," wrote Leslie Fiedler, "is not the confrontation with the alien landscape . . . but the encounter with the Indian, that utter stranger for whom our New World is an Old Home."

One of Frederic Remington's last major paintings, *The Love Call* (opposite), shows a peaceful aspect of Indian life, as a suitor plays a serenade on his reed pipe to attract a woman from the camp beyond. This graceful individual, clad in simple robes, blends into his surroundings with the confidence of someone who has inhabited them for centuries.

Most Hollywood movies, on the other hand, painted the Indian in harsh pejorative colors, as a savage enemy to be defeated and swept aside by the inexorable westward movement of white Americans. Even as late as *The Searchers* (1956), John Ford's films generally depict Indians with similar broad strokes. There are exceptions, however, and Ford was also capable of showing the hostility and bigotry of whites toward Native Americans in a surprising light. Some of this ambivalence and complexity is evident in *The Searchers* and in the conflicted character of Ethan Edwards: his extended hunt for the Indians who abducted his niece and slaughtered the rest of her family turns into obsession in the grip of bloodlust. When Martin Pawley, his companion on the long trail, draws the poison from Ethan's arrow wound as the latter lies in a cave, he is, as J. A. Place has written, "cleansing him of his hatred but also of Indian malignancy." Pawley himself is a half-caste, taunted by Ethan and made ridiculous by the sturdy "squaw" who follows him from a Comanche camp. A prisoner of both races, Pawley gradually becomes a symbol of hope for the future, a conciliatory figure who stands between Ethan and his lust for vengeance against the Comanche.

In *The Searchers,* the pre-Custer cavalry plays a subordinate and by no means flattering role. During the final third of the film, the familiar sound of the charge streaks across a snow-covered landscape, as Ethan vents his frustration by gunning down as many buffalo as possible. But this time the cavalrymen appear not as rescuers but as captors, leading a huddled procession of Comanche across the plains to the nearest fort. The only representative of the cavalry to appear in close-up, as it were, is one Lieutenant Greenhill (John Wayne's son Patrick), an inexperienced, somewhat boneheaded youth who clearly owes his commission to his father, Colonel Greenhill (shades of *Rio Grande*). Ford mocks the lad's clumsy handling of his saber and, by extension, the insensitivity of the military toward all things native and unfamiliar.

The Indian population had been forced to retreat to the North and West from the early decades of the nineteenth century, though Thomas Cole (1801–1848) still enjoyed showing an Indian warrior beside the falls in his important painting *Landscape with Tree Trunks* (1828). Within three years, the great French historian Alexis de Tocqueville would declare with chilling foresight: "I believe that the Indian race of North America is condemned to perish, and I don't doubt when the day comes when Europeans will be established on the shores of the Pacific Ocean, that race will cease to exist."

A generation later, Francis Parkman offered an almost ethnographic description of various tribes, particularly the "Dahcotah" (dubbed "Sioux" by earlier French explorers and trappers—their version of a Chippewa word for snake or foe). He noted their lack of "fixed habitation," something that perplexed the European pioneer and also worries John Wayne's characters in films such as *She Wore a Yellow Ribbon* and *The Searchers*. In their work, artists sought to evoke the nomadic warrior. For example, Cyrus Dallin's eloquent bronze *On the Warpath* (opposite) shows an Indian brave staring backward, relaxed in his bareback posture, with the feather of merit rising proudly from his headband.

"Hunting and fighting," declares Parkman, "they wander incessantly, through summer and winter. Some are following the herds of buffalo over the waste of

Cyrus Dallin. *On the Warpath*. 1914. Bronze, 41¾ x 41½ x 13". Rockwell Museum of Western Art, Corning, New York

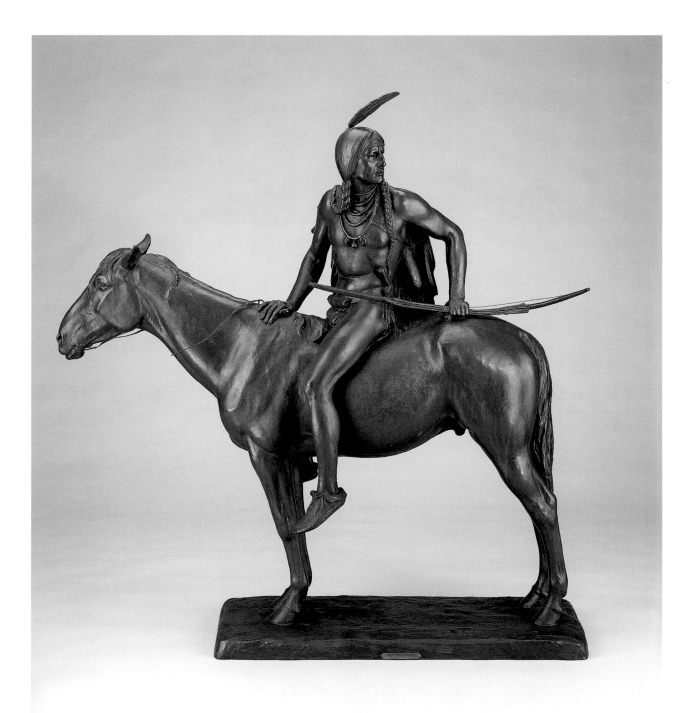

prairie; others are traversing the Black Hills, thronging, on horseback and on foot, through the dark gulfs and sombre gorges, beneath the vast splintering precipices, and emerging at last upon the 'Parks,' those beautiful but most perilous hunting-grounds. The buffalo supplies them with almost all the necessities of life; with habitations, food, clothing, and fuel; with strings for their bows, with thread, cordage and trailropes for their horses, with coverings for their saddles, with vessels to hold water, with boats to cross streams, with glue, and with the means of purchasing all that they desire from the traders." Charles M. Russell captured the confrontational force of the Native American's struggle with the buffalo in his painting *Indians Hunting Buffalo* (opposite): the doomed creature charges, head down like a bull in the ring, oblivious to the fate about to strike it in the form of the warrior's arrow.

Settlers, cattlemen, prospectors, and soldiers alike regarded the Indian tribes as a ferocious adversary standing in the way of the westward expansion of whites. By the early 1880s, after decades of sometimes bloody confrontation, only about a quarter of a million Native Americans remained, roughly 25 percent of their population in the early eighteenth century. As Ford highlights in *She Wore a Yellow Ribbon,* numerous tribes came together in the wake of the Indian triumph at the Little Big Horn—with, as the film's narrator puts it, "signal smokes, war drums, feathered bonnet against the Western sky. New messiahs, young leaders are ready to hurl the finest light cavalry in the world against Fort Starke." In their efforts to recover their traditional hunting grounds, longtime enemies temporarily forgot their differences to unite in a common cause. But impetuous tactics in the face of an increasingly well-marshaled U.S. Army soon destroyed that dream. Sitting Bull and his band of Sioux were obliged to seek exile in Canada. In 1881, close to starvation, Sitting Bull surrendered to the U.S. authorities and became, in effect, a prisoner of war at the Standing Rock Reservation. Soon he was recruited by Buffalo Bill's Wild West Show, where he sat in lone splendor signing photographs of himself at a dollar a print. Russell's painting *Buffalo Bill's Duel with Yellowhand* (1917) celebrates the victory of the white man, with the Indian already beaten and about to join a cow's skeleton in the stream that forever divides him from the triumphant Bill.

Charles M. Russell.
*Indians Hunting Buffalo
(Wild Men's Meat,
Buffalo Hunt)*. 1894. Oil
on canvas, 24⅛ x 36⅛".
Courtesy Sid Richardson
Collection of Western
Art, Fort Worth, Texas

Native American Actors

Of all the Native Americans whom John Ford employed in his films, Chief John Big Tree (1865–1967) is the most noteworthy. He started his screen career in 1915, at the age of fifty, and would live to become a centenarian. He appeared in Ford's early Western *A Fight for Love* (1919), then in *The Iron Horse* five years later. In *Stagecoach* (1939) he played (uncredited) an Indian scout, and in *Drums Along the Mohawk* (also 1939) he portrayed Blue Back, the taciturn but good-hearted Iroquois clad in a blanket and an incongruous three-cornered hat embellished with a distinctive single feather. His final appearance for Ford was in *She Wore a Yellow Ribbon* (1949), as the sane, wise Chief Pony That Walks (opposite), who greets his old friend Captain Nathan Brittles with the pipe of peace while younger braves threaten conflict. "Come with me and hunt buffalo," he cries, "smoke many pipes," adding, "We are too old for war." Nathan responds that "old men should stop wars." But for Pony That Walks, it is "too late." He prefers the notion of getting drunk together with his "brother," Nathan, and presents him with an embroidered scarf. Without underlining the parallel, Ford renders this scene as an emotional counterpart to Nathan's receiving his silver watch from the troop at Fort Starke.

As with most other Hollywood movies until recent years, Ford did not always cast Native American parts authentically. His most menacing "Indian" was in fact a German character actor born in Berlin. Henry Brandon (1912–1990) reveled in the malevolent characters of Scar in *The Searchers* (1956) and Quanah Parker in *Two Rode Together* (1961).

Posed production photo from *She Wore a Yellow Ribbon*, with Chief John Big Tree and Joanne Dru

A title in the 1913 silent film *The Friendless Indian* reads: "Condemned to walk alone, a Red Man saves a life and is given only a nod of thanks—after all, he is Indian." Even when the movies were not being completely hostile, Hollywood's attitude toward the Native American could be summed up in that single sentence. In the second decade of the twentieth century, some Indians gravitated toward Hollywood; among them was Chief Dark Cloud, who appeared in D. W. Griffith's *Song of the Wildwood Flute* in 1910. Even so, as early as 1914, Alanson Skinner, assistant curator of the Department of Anthropology at the American Museum of Natural History, was protesting to the *New York Times*: "From the standpoint of a student, most of the picture plays shown are ethnologically grotesque farces. Delawares are dressed as Sioux, and the Indians of Manhattan island are shown dwelling in skin tipis of the type used only by the tribes beyond the Mississippi." According to Kevin Brownlow, however, Skinner and other authorities were united in their commendation of F. E. Moore's 1913 epic, *Hiawatha,* performed by "one hundred and fifty full-blooded Indians, with photography by Victor Milner."

A handful of early films treated the "red man" with respect. Brownlow has noted that "Rodman Wanamaker's *History of the American Indian* ran thirteen reels, an unusually ambitious length for 1915. Directed by Rollin S. Dixon, it was a careful documentary record of rites and ceremonies that were already forgotten by young Indians." There was even an Indian director, James Young Deer (or Youngdeer, as he later styled himself). A member of the Winnebago tribe, Youngdeer directed documentaries about his people as well as Westerns for Pathé Frères on the West Coast.

From the outset, John Ford used authentic Native Americans in his films and encouraged them to arrive for work wearing their traditional tribal clothes and decorations. He recruited scores of Cheyenne, Sioux, and Pawnee men for *The Iron Horse* (1924), which shows the Indians charging at the railroad workers and locomotives time and again in an attempt to turn the tide of progress. Despite the touches of authenticity, Ford's treatment of Native Americans was often like that of other directors, disparaging and negative, although there are noteworthy distinctions.

On most occasions, Ford's films refer to Indian atrocities in dialogue or implicitly, rather than showing them in close-up. In *Fort Apache* (1948), after Mescalero Apache have attacked a repair wagon, Lieutenant O'Rourke reports he found two troopers "spread-eagled on the wheel . . . roasted." The final slaughter of Colonel Thursday and his few remaining troopers is conveyed by a combination of sound and almost abstract imagery, with the overwhelming noise of the Indians galloping down the canyon over long shots obscured by the dust kicked up from the desert floor. When the Indians turn on the crooked sutler in *She Wore a Yellow Ribbon* (page 132), they throw him and his men into a blazing fire, while Captain Brittles watches from the rocks above, unable to intervene. All he can do is chew on a big plug of tobacco and offer a "chaw" to his companions in hiding, Sergeant Tyree and Lieutenant Pennell. The savagery, shown only briefly but quite audible, is essentially conveyed in Brittles's stoic gaze. He has seen such things before, but for the younger soldiers at his side the horror comes as a shock. In *The Searchers,* the viciousness of the Comanche is manifested through the gestures and words of Ethan Edwards, in the scene when he returns from a dark canyon and, little by little but never too explicitly, describes finding young Lucy's body there and leaving his coat to cover her. When Brad—Lucy's beau—asks him for more information about what had happened to Lucy, Ethan almost loses control. "D'you want me to draw you a picture?" he barks. "Never ask me more!"

The flavor and dread of frontier life are more vividly communicated in *Drums Along the Mohawk* (1939), set in the frontier of pre-Revolutionary upper New York, than in the more celebrated *Stagecoach,* made less than a year earlier and set in the Southwest of the late nineteenth century. *Drums Along the Mohawk* features the Five Nations of the Iroquois, as had Griffith's epic *America* some fifteen years earlier, and as Cecil B. DeMille's *Unconquered* would do in 1947. Ford exploits the pioneers' unfamiliarity with Indians to dramatic and sometimes even witty effect. When the Mohawk Blue Back emerges suddenly from the dark shadows of Gilbert's cabin, the freshly married Lana goes into hysterics. The fact that Blue Back is a stalwart friend of Gil's, and refuses to join the perfidious English in the colonial wars, only slightly diminishes his sinister authority.

OPPOSITE
*She Wore a Yellow
Ribbon:* Paul Fix and
Harry Woods as
gunrunners about to be
roasted alive by their
customers

The Indians set fire to
the sheaves in *Drums
Along the Mohawk.*

In *Drums Along the Mohawk,* Ford depicts the hostile Iroquois as shrewd, calculating, and ruthless in their attacks on the settlers and their dwellings. They prefer to instill sufficient panic in their enemies to make the settlers evacuate their farms, before the Indians advance from the surrounding woodland and put the buildings to the torch (below). The film also features one of the most brilliantly shot and edited sequences in the Ford canon, showing Gil Martin being pursued by three implacable Iroquois braves as he runs to a distant fort beneath a vast, angry sky.

Ford depicts the white man's bigotry in his films too. That prejudice is by no means limited to Native Americans—for example, Wyatt Earp's barely disguised

aversion to the "half-breed" Chihuahua in *My Darling Clementine* hints at deep-seated prejudice—but it plumbs the nadir in the treatment of Indians in *Fort Apache*. Lieutenant Colonel Owen Thursday—not at all a sympathetic character—reviles the Apache at every opportunity, describing them as "cowardly digger Indians." When Captain Kirby York protests that he has given his word that Cochise will not be harmed if he crosses back into Arizona from Mexico, Thursday sneers: "Your word to a breech-clouted savage . . . an illiterate, uncivilized murderer and treaty-breaker. There's no question of honor between an American officer and Cochise."

Ford never shirks from exposing stupidity, and in this film even the habitual discipline of the U.S. Cavalry seems to have deserted Colonel Thursday and his troopers. It is the Indians who calculate their assault and who fire in ranks from among the rocks, with a methodical discipline normally observed by the cavalry. As Collingwood, the colonel's old comrade-in-arms, warns Thursday, Cochise has "out-generaled us, out-fought us, and out-run us" in six campaigns over the previous three years.

Before his final attack, Cochise (Miguel Inclan), dignified in the face of Thursday's scorn, utters one of the most rousing statements spoken by a Native American in Ford's work. "The Apache are a great race," he proclaims. "We have never been conquered." Yet, he continues, it is not good always to be fighting, for the young men die, the women weep, and the old go hungry in the winter. He condemns Meacham, the trader sent by the U.S. government to provide the Apache with supplies—and, illicitly, weapons (opposite). "We will not return to your reservation while men like him are there," he declares. And, unfazed by the squadron of cavalry arrayed against him, he boasts, "For each one of us that you kill, ten white men will die." Still, in a tone of regret and melancholy, Cochise acknowledges the destiny of his people: "We looked to the white man for protection—but he gave us slow death." Stubborn officers like Owen Thursday do not realize that their arrogance toward the Native American plays into the hands of hotheaded young braves like Geronimo and Diablo—or Red Shirt in *Cheyenne Autumn*, to take another example.

John Wayne, Grant Withers (as the Indian trader, Meacham), and Henry Fonda in *Fort Apache*

Even after the massacre of Thursday's command, Cochise shows his magnanimity when he stops short of also slaughtering Captain York, previously ordered to move some distance away and stay with the supply train. When York unbuckles his gun belt and advances toward him in a mood of surrender, Cochise simply hurls the captured regimental guidon into the sand and rides away with all his warriors, leaving the captain humiliated in a scurry of dust.

Occasionally, there was a respite from the mutual enmity. In *Wagon Master,* the Indians remain in the background, happy to dance with the Mormon settlers as they trundle through Indian territory. But in *Rio Grande* (opposite), shot six months after *Wagon Master,* the Apache are portrayed as drunken and unpredictable, pouncing on an unprotected wagon train, raping and killing a trooper's wife, seizing white children as hostages, and invoking a punitive attack by the cavalry on an unprepared Indian encampment. The screenplay by James Kevin McGuinness does not attempt to conceal its right-wing, racist stance. "C'est sauvage. Barbare," whispers Captain St. Jacques (Peter Ortiz), as he contemplates the corpse of the murdered woman (although Ford, ever discreet, does not show the outrage on screen). Joseph Breen, director of the Production Code Administration, urged Ford to make cuts in the screenplay, including such lines as "These Apaches are the only Indians who kill and torture for the sheer lust of it." In the paranoid anti-Communist mood of the early 1950s, Joseph McBride believes, Ford probably regarded the "Red Indians" more as "Reds" than as Indians. Nevertheless, even to the Spanish conquistadores hundreds of years earlier, the Apache seemed to be the most vicious and lethal of foes in the American Southwest. The very name "Apache" was a Spanish form of the Zuni word for "enemy." Justified or not, the Apache were dealt some of the harshest treatment of any Native American peoples in films.

Rio Grande: The wagon is pushed over to form a barrier behind which the soldiers can take shelter and fire against the onrushing Indians.

The Searchers has long been characterized as Ford's most bitter film, with Ethan Edwards as a man diverted from vengeance only at the last gasp. It's true that John Wayne's characterization hisses and burns with a corrosive anger—an anger that is purged only by his scalping of Scar. His hooded, sidewinder glare and his defensive refrain—"That'll be the day!"—give way at last to one of the cinema's most poignant lines: "Let's go home, Debbie." The origins of his resentment may be found in the Civil War, which concluded only three years prior to the beginning of the story. Ethan, wearing the distinctive red shirt of the Confederacy, refused to surrender, and now, still embittered by defeat, he bestows his medal on his little niece Debbie—only to see it dangling from the neck of Scar later in the film. Yet this is also a man who has sought to comprehend the Indian culture. He has learned much of their tribal language. When he fires at the corpse of the Comanche brave, it is because he knows that if "he got no eyes, he has to wander forever, between the winds."

Still, the more one sees the film, the more readily apparent are its lighter moments too. The hilarious circumstances of Martin Pawley's "marriage" to a plump, beaming squaw provoke amusement, along with recognition of Ethan's knowledge of Comanche customs. The rivalry and fisticuffs between Marty and the inane Charlie McCorry (Ken Curtis) for the hand of Laurie Jorgensen gives the drama a buoyancy that sustains one's faith in the Fordian family concept. So too does the bickering between Ward Bond's Reverend Sam and John Wayne's Ethan, hovering as it does, dangerously, on the verge of outright hostility.

The Jorgensen homestead in *The Searchers* appears rather ridiculous, because there are scarcely any grazing grounds in Monument Valley, and the house itself could not be more exposed. The same applies to the Edwards cabin. In fact, Henry Nash Smith has pointed out that by the mid-1870s, "lands were being taken up in areas where the rainfall was likely to decline every few years below the level necessary for the traditional type of farming on which the myth of the 'garden' had been based." Besides, Monument Valley forms an organic part of the settlers' lives in *The Searchers*. Two gravestones behind the Edwards dwelling bear testimony to an earlier generation of pioneers, and the need to set down roots. So too do the copper pans and pewter plates arrayed above the mantel in the Jorgensen parlor, along with the cherished "Sweden chest" that embodies memories of a distant civilization. "Gotta fetch her home," says Marty in a dull, obstinate tone when he leaves the doting Laurie to pursue the quest for Debbie. "Home" is the magic word that justifies the very existence of these settlers. "Oh, Ethan, this country, . . ." says Lars Jorgensen (John Qualen) as he remembers his son Brad, now dead, and his voice succumbs to emotion. In that lament lies an infinite regret for a virgin land tinged with fear of both Native Americans and the ruthless nature of the terrain.

Yet both Ethan Edwards and the Reverend Sam recognize their ties to the desert and its outlandish monuments. Sam remains at ease in a rugged society where in the space of a few seconds, his Confederate's shirt can be replaced by the frock coat, starched shirtfront, and black tie of a reverend ready to perform the marriage rites. Doc Holliday in *My Darling Clementine* may harbor memories of a world beyond the valley; not so Ethan Edwards, or the Jorgensens, or Martin Pawley. They are condemned to journey, as on a leash, from one extreme of the landscape to another (page 141), attempting to preserve their own skin while seeking the soul of a single survivor—Debbie—who can justify their way of life.

If, at the end, Ethan turns away in the light beyond the homestead door, it is because, like the dead Comanche, he is sentenced by destiny to return to the dust and the rocks, to dwell in exile beyond the perimeter of civilized settlements, "to wander forever between the winds." Outraged by the savagery of the Comanche, he himself must bear the shame of a people as violent as their foes and, where Jerem Futterman the "trader" is concerned, every bit as treacherous.

The Plains Indians bestowed the sobriquet "Buffalo Soldiers" on the cavalrymen of African-American descent who were dispatched to the Western frontier in the years following the Civil War. *Sergeant Rutledge* (1960) deals with some of the issues arising from that curious decision, and the film was apparently inspired by a Remington study of black cavalrymen. The artist much admired the physique of these soldiers

OPPOSITE
Frederic Remington.
The Luckless Hunter.
1909. Oil on canvas,
26⅞ x 28⅞". Courtesy
Sid Richardson
Collection of Western
Art, Fort Worth, Texas

Jeffrey Hunter and John
Wayne ride grimly
through the snow in *The
Searchers*.

("great chests, broad-shouldered, upstanding fellows") as well as their courage. He had made sketches of several such cavalrymen of the Ninth and Tenth Cavalry Regiments (United States Colored Troops) on a visit to Arizona in 1888.

Sergeant Rutledge again underlines wanton savagery by the Indians: the body of young Chris Hubble is discovered in broad daylight, staked out for vultures to circle over. This film makes an intriguing parallel between the black man and the Indian. Both are regarded with fear by the whites, not just because of the hue of their skin but also because of a perceived physical superiority. Woody Strode's Rutledge startles the demure young Mary Beecher (Constance Towers) when he clamps a conspicuously black hand over her mouth like some Hitchcock villain: "It was as though he had sprung up at me out of the earth," she tells Rutledge's court-martial later. During the long sequence by night at the isolated Spindle Station, with the wind tearing in from the desert, Mary Beecher seems to be as much in dread of Rutledge as she is of the Apache lurking unseen beyond the shelter of the station building. Some of the sergeant's lines could come from the mouths of Indians: "White women only spell trouble for any of us." Strode, incidentally, had Creek and Blackfoot blood, as well as being African-American.

The screenplay by James Warner Bellah and Willis Goldbeck tends to patronize the figure of Rutledge. Thanks to Strode's noble bearing and his intelligent acting, the character in the film assumes a dignity that the often prejudiced Bellah in particular could never have allowed him. Ford emphasizes this with the very first shot of Strode, as he strides out of the somber shadows of the fort's terrace, resplendent in his uniform and towering over the guards who flank him.

The prejudice against Native Americans is made only slightly less distasteful by the facetious antics of the court-martial. The presiding colonel takes repeated swigs from a "water" jug that actually contains raw whiskey (the same harsh brew, no doubt, that Rutledge needs to treat his wounds after the Apache attack). The colonel's wife, all prim in bonnet and crinoline and carrying a parasol, asks if the Bible she must swear on is in fact the "Authorized Version." She also embarrasses her husband by reminding him that the china clock in their home was the one he

Constance Towers and Woody Strode in *Sergeant Rutledge*

had stolen while his men were sacking Atlanta in the Civil War. In an ultimate flippancy, the court is adjourned to allow the committee to indulge in a game of poker.

Ford's acknowledgment of the inequities of frontier life may be felt in the final remark by Lieutenant Cantrell (Jeffrey Hunter) to Mary Beecher: "It's a good land. Maybe not now. But, like Rutledge says—someday."

Two Rode Together (1961), in many ways a remake of *The Searchers,* again focuses on the rescue of a white woman captured and sexually initiated by the Native American. The later film contains few references to the Civil War, but Richard Widmark's First Lieutenant Jim Gary exemplifies the calm and reasoned officer Ford clearly admired. (There are echoes of *Fort Apache* in the formal officers' dance, as Widmark, in the full panoply of cavalry uniform, waltzes with Linda Cristal's Elena.) His susceptibilities are tested to the limit by James Stewart's amiable but corrupt Marshal Guthrie McCabe, who breathes the same bitter and vituperative opinions as Wayne's character in *The Searchers.*

When drunk, the marshal seems to take sadistic pleasure in telling Shirley Jones's Marty Purcell how her little brother must have grown up to become a Comanche, repulsive and attuned to the killing of whites. More macho than any man in Ford's Western output, McCabe treats white "squaw" captives and the unfortunate Marty with equal scorn and distaste. When Henry Brandon's Chief Quanah Parker (opposite) pursues the white men, he must be dispatched before he can penetrate the protective circle of light cast by McCabe's and Lieutenant Gary's fire.

Ford, however, allows Hanna Clegg (played by an uncredited Mae Marsh) to account for her reluctance to rejoin white society after living for years as a prisoner among the Comanche. He also underscores the crass reaction of officers and their wives alike when confronted by Elena, a freed "squaw" captive, at the formal dance. Approaching her, one obtuse woman from the fort asks, "Among the savages, is it true that . . . ?" Yet nothing can wash *Two Rode Together* clean of its prejudice against miscegenation, and the film lacks the purgative redemption of a line like "Let's go home, Debbie," in *The Searchers.*

Dealing in guns: Woody Strode, James Stewart, Richard Widmark, and Henry Brandon in *Two Rode Together*

James Stewart

Having spent the 1950s making a series of harsh, ambivalent Westerns for Anthony Mann and serving as a leading man for Alfred Hitchcock, James Stewart (1908–1997) ambled into John Ford's final three Westerns to jocular effect (below). His wry, tongue-in-cheek personality contrasted with the self-conscious decency of Richard Widmark in *Two Rode Together* (1961) and *Cheyenne Autumn* (1964), and with John

James Stewart (seen here in *Two Rode Together*) came late to the Ford troupe, in the wake of several Westerns directed by Anthony Mann.

Wayne's dour efficiency in *The Man Who Shot Liberty Valance* (1962). Ford knew how to bring out the guile in Stewart, that deceptively sleepy wariness that in turn leads to an obstinate pursuit of his quarry. In *Two Rode Together,* he can sit at the river's edge alongside Widmark, puffing on a cigar and engaging in easy banter during a take of almost four minutes; however, once wooed from his comfortable, semi-corrupt retirement as town marshal, he must search for a group of white captives already held for several years by the Comanche. The

Ford (at left) with James Stewart on location for *Two Rode Together*

"Did that look good?"
Ford with John Wayne
and James Stewart
on location for *The
Man Who Shot Liberty
Valance*

quest to some degree recalls Ethan's in *The Searchers* (and both characters speak passable Comanche). Stewart's character is equally embittered, if more mercenary. At the end, he may ride off with his woman toward the promise of California, but he has lost his post as marshal and looms as nothing more than a poor man's Shane.

In *The Man Who Shot Liberty Valance,* Ford gives Stewart a role altogether less self-assured. Tall and grave, the distinguished senator from "Capitol City" (the state is unidentified) comes home to the soporific town of Shinbone to expiate his guilt—at having assumed the halo of a hero, and the commitment of a loving wife, at the expense of his old friend Tom Doniphon, who has just died. In the flashbacks that constitute most of the film, Stewart portrays the younger Ransom Stoddard with a judicious blend of the zeal of an attorney and the susceptibility of a novice. Throughout the film, humiliated though he is by the taunting of Liberty Valance and the gentler chiding of Doniphon, Stoddard maintains an air of grace under pressure. Ford finds his character engaging because Stoddard rejects the eye-for-an-eye doctrine of the Old West. The film satirizes such hallowed precepts as the courageous marshal (in the gross and craven figure of Andy Devine's Link Appleyard) and the triumph of good over evil in a climactic, fair gunfight. When his reading and writing class is summarily canceled as a result of Doniphon's intervention, Stoddard turns to the blackboard and wipes off his maxim "Education is the basis of Law and Order."

Cheyenne Autumn offers Stewart a juicy smaller role as Wyatt Earp in Dodge City (page 150). The episode has absolutely nothing to do with the focus of the film, the plight of the Indians in their flight from the U.S. Cavalry, and Stewart's characterization stands at a far remove from Fonda's Earp in *My Darling Clementine*. Like some Shakespearean comic interlude, this little cadenza by Ford relieves the enveloping gloom of the narrative, while also satirizing the heroic image of the Old West. Stewart merely has to chew on his cigar and command a poker game with reptilian vigilance. No other actor would have dared conspire with Ford in such a subversive attack on the hallowed lineaments of the Western genre. Like Ford himself by then, this Wyatt Earp is as "blind as a bat," and equally contemptuous of the mob mentality that the director had derided as long ago as in *Young Mr. Lincoln*.

The Dodge City sequence in *Cheyenne Autumn,* with Arthur Kennedy, James Stewart, and Elizabeth Allen

Ford saw *Cheyenne Autumn* (1964) as an opportunity to redress the balance of his career in favor of the Native American. "I've killed more Indians than Custer, Beecher, and Chivington put together," he conceded, "and people in Europe always want to know about the Indians. . . . Let's face it, we've treated them very badly—it's a blot on our shield; we've cheated and robbed, killed, murdered, massacred and everything else, but they kill one white man and God, out come the troops." The nineteenth-century novelist Emerson Bennett wrote of "trappers [who], to the horror of the genteel hero Frank Leighton, delight in scalping Indians," and there are characters like that in Ford's films. Owen Thursday in *Fort Apache* certainly hates the Indians with a impassioned fury, and the vengeful Ethan Edwards in *The Searchers* takes to scalping.

Cheyenne Autumn is a sad, sympathetic film in which Ford looks at events more from the perspective of the Indians than in any of his previous movies (page 152). The year is 1878, and at the start the cavalry has a muted, thankless role; more like United Nations peacekeepers, the troopers must function with their hands figuratively tied. The atrocities are not entirely finished; the nightmare of Wounded Knee, with the Sioux brought to their knees for the last time, still lies a dozen years in the future. But this time anyway, it seems, the cavalry may no longer simply cut a swath through Indian villages and torch the nearest tepees.

In previous years, the Cheyenne had proved to be among the most obdurate opponents that the U.S. Army encountered. Remington's bronze *The Cheyenne* (page 154) personifies the power and grace of the warrior, with rider and horse wedded in motion, focused relentlessly on the attack. The Southern Cheyenne resisted the U.S. Cavalry until they were overwhelmed in the Red River War of 1874–75. The Northern Cheyenne joined forces with the Sioux and took part in the Battle of the Little Big Horn in 1876. They were routed by a vengeful cavalry in the aftermath of Custer's demise, then penned up in a reservation in Oklahoma (which Ford filmed in Monument Valley, of course). But toward the end of 1878, they spontaneously, and with great dignity, decided to trek fifteen hundred miles to the north, back to Yellowstone and their traditional homeland.

Sal Mineo, Nancy
Hseuh, and Dolores Del
Rio in *Cheyenne Autumn*

According to the historian Dee Brown, during the night of September 9, 1878, Little Wolf and Dull Knife "told their people to pack and be ready to start at first daylight. They left their tepees standing empty behind them and headed northward across the sand hills—297 men, women, and children." Less than a third of them were warriors, and there were not enough horses to carry everyone. More than ten thousand soldiers from various forts, accompanied by three thousand other whites, eventually joined the pursuit. One should not forget—and Ford surely did not forget—that the particular "long march" described in *Cheyenne Autumn* not only was based on a true story but also was a condensation of many, many such treks, forced and unforced. The Delaware, the Chiricahua Apache (under Geronimo), the Chickasaw, the Seminole of Florida, and—most notoriously—the Cherokee were among the Indian nations driven away to the reservation areas of the Great Plains and Far West during the nineteenth century.

In *Cheyenne Autumn,* Ford also focuses on two types of soldier. Richard Widmark's Captain Archer represents the hidebound past, with his conviction that the Cheyenne are "meaner than sin"; but as the film progresses, he begins to acknowledge the incompetence and bureaucracy of federal policy toward the Indians, while his affection for a local schoolteacher (Carroll Baker) who works with the Cheyenne softens the edge of his racism. On the other hand, Karl Malden's Captain Wessels—a Prussian immigrant, who appears in the final third of the film—represents the worst element in the military, with his ungovernable rages and his ingrained hatred of the Indians. Speaking with a Germanic accent and wearing a Hitlerian mustache, Wessels refuses to question the chain of command. "What would this world be without orders—uh?" he demands in a drunken stupor. If blame for the loss of life among both the cavalry and the Cheyenne in the final frenzied struggle in the snow can be laid at Wessels's door, one can also see this benighted officer as a product of army discipline and years of relentless training in hostile terrain.

At the end of *Cheyenne Autumn,* the handful of surviving Indians gather defiantly at Victory Cave, Dakota Territory. In many respects, the cavalry has suffered

Frederic Remington.
The Cheyenne. 1901.
Bronze, 19¾ x 23½ x
9". Rockwell Museum of
Art, Corning, New York

an even greater blow to its pride. Throughout the film, Ford deliberately presents the cavalry as vulnerable and brittle in the sturdy immensity of the Far West. The troopers ride in lines of two abreast, more fearful of Cheyenne willfulness than of any fresh, traditional attack by whooping warriors from the flanks. While the Cheyenne walk through the landscape as though familiar with every dune and boulder, the soldiers seem like unnerved voyagers to an alien planet, making sudden, irresolute forays in their efforts to keep in touch with their former internees.

Ford arrives at something approaching a reconciliation between the cavalry and the Native American in the closing scenes of *Cheyenne Autumn,* as Captain Archer receives the implicit surrender of the last remaining Cheyenne and ushers them back to their reservation. Was Ford thinking of his idol, General Douglas MacArthur, accepting the Japanese surrender in Tokyo Bay in 1945? Even if that is the case, *Cheyenne Autumn* departs from Ford's habitual view of the cavalry as a noble profession full of bugles and banter, instead disclosing the asperity of army existence and the exasperation of its officers when awaiting the arrival of the latest congressional committee. As Captain Collingwood says wearily in *Fort Apache,* "This isn't a country for glory."

Mari Sandoz, author of the original novel on which *Cheyenne Autumn* was based, expressed her disappointment with the film in an Associated Press interview in 1965: "They made it slow and dreadful, and this was a story of a great pursuit. I don't see how you can make a slow story about one of the great chases of history. They made it dull." On the contrary, the deliberate movements in *Cheyenne Autumn* serve as counterpoint to the dozens of frantic, whooping Indian attacks that Ford had filmed through the decades. His Cheyenne here behave with a natural dignity, reaching a climax with the passing of the "sacred bundle" from Little Wolf to the younger Dull Knife. *Cheyenne Autumn* heralded a whole range of "psychological" Westerns, films that sacrificed the traditional fast pace of the genre for long, brooding moments of reflection and analysis.

In his own autumn, Ford would declare: "Who better than an Irishman could understand the Indians, while still being stirred by tales of the U.S. Cavalry? We were on both sides of the epic." In defense of Ford's approach to the Native American issue, one can say that he responded to the romantic reading of his youth. Like millions of other red-blooded Americans, he thrived on every line of James Fenimore Cooper, and probably Henry Wadsworth Longfellow's poem *Hiawatha* as well. Ford's Westerns helped nourish the myth of a stark, unyielding frontier land that marked the jagged line between civilization and barbarity. Ethan Edwards in *The Searchers* has much of Leatherstocking's innate violence, along with his inability to dwell in "civilized" society. In fact, Ford found much to admire in the older generation—Pony That Walks in *She Wore a Yellow Ribbon,* Cochise in *Fort Apache*—as well as the impetuous younger generation of braves such as Scar in *The Searchers* or Red Shirt (Sal Mineo) in *Cheyenne Autumn*. Ford would have had difficulty directing a film such as Elliot Silverstein's *A Man Called Horse* (1970), with its patronizing attitude toward Indian customs and "barbarity." At the same time, even though he shows a soldier in *Cheyenne Autumn* scalping an Indian for little reason other than vexation, Ford could never have treated his beloved Bluecoats with such sulfurous irony as Arthur Penn does in *Little Big Man*.

Like Frederic Remington, Ford found that the Native American exhibited a "nobility of purpose" in defeat, and sympathy and respect increasingly marked the director's attitude toward a vanquished foe. After successfully stampeding the Indian pony herd in *She Wore a Yellow Ribbon,* Captain Nathan Brittles tells his troopers to follow the braves as they return on foot to their reservation—but a mile to the rear. "Walking hurts their pride," he say gently, "and your watching them will make it worse."

Charles M. Russell. *In the Enemy's Country*. 1921. Oil on canvas, 24 x 36". Denver Art Museum Collection. Gift of the Magness Family in memory of Betsy Magness, 1991.751

Stagecoach: Followed
by a cavalry escort,
the stagecoach crosses

CHAPTER 5

MONUMENT VALLEY AND FORD'S EXPANSIVE VISION OF THE WEST

The credit sequence for *Stagecoach* lasts but a brisk seventy seconds, yet it constitutes an altogether new departure for the Western—and the first use of Monument Valley in John Ford's career. The essential elements that would mark his greatest work in the genre are there behind the credits: the coach and the cavalry detachment that follows in protective attendance, the Indians who loom out of the twilight, and the immense skies above the buttes and mesas of Monument Valley itself.

How did Ford come upon this extraordinary location in southeastern Utah and northeastern Arizona? And how did he give its overwhelming physical grandeur such a heroic dimension, to the point that no director in Hollywood dared to trespass in Monument Valley, for fear of being accused of "plagiarizing" John Ford? Prior to *Stagecoach* in 1939, only one Western, George B. Seitz's *The Vanishing American* (1925), had shown Monument Valley as a backdrop. That film had been based on a story by the legendary Western author Zane Grey, who conceived it during a visit to the valley as early as 1913.

The place to stay when visiting Monument Valley is Goulding's Lodge, founded some years after Harry Goulding discovered the valley and succumbed to its awesome spell. In 1922, the area formed part of the Paiute Indian reservation, and private ownership of land was forbidden. But within twelve months, the Paiute (who had lost their own homelands in the nineteenth century) had moved their reservation; the valley passed into public domain, and Harry Goulding paid a derisory $320 in 1923 for a stretch of 640 square acres in the shadow of Big Rock Door Mesa, at the northwestern tip of the valley.

In the words of Michael F. Blake, Goulding was "a tall, lanky cowboy in the style of Gary Cooper, hailing from Colorado." In fact, he was more at home with sheep-herding, and he quickly learned to live off the land like the Navajo in the vicinity, who numbered about one hundred thousand. The Navajo greeted the newcomers with suspicion, but that soon changed to respect and finally to affection, especially after the Gouldings' trading post enabled them to secure items of food and clothing that had long been beyond their reach.

Daily life, however, proved harsher and less exotic than it appears to the casual visitor today. To quote Ford's grandson Dan, "Malnutrition, disease, unemployment, and alcoholism were the four horsemen of the Navajo's apocalypse." By 1938, in the trough of the Great Depression, the Indians' economy had languished to the point that the opportunistic Goulding knew he had to take drastic action. Hearing from John Wetherill, a neighbor at Kayenta (not far south of Monument Valley), that Hollywood scouts were in Flagstaff, Arizona, looking for suitable locations for a new Western to be directed by John Ford, Goulding quickly prepared a portfolio of images by the German photographer Josef Muench. Accompanied by his wife, Leone (known as "Mike"), Goulding arrived in Los Angeles by train and somehow bluffed his way into United Artists and the offices of John Ford and his producer, Walter Wanger. Stunned by the Muench photographs, Ford and Wanger agreed within hours to use Monument Valley as the principal location for *Stagecoach*.

Ford and the Navajo

For his extras and Indians of every hue and tribe, Ford turned to the Navajo indigenous to Monument Valley. They played Arapaho and Apache in *She Wore a Yellow Ribbon,* Comanche in *The Searchers,* and Cheyenne in *Cheyenne Autumn.* The actor Iron Eyes Cody (1907–1999) recalled how the Navajo in Monument Valley had been severely undermined by a succession of bad winters when Ford decided to make *Stagecoach* there (opposite). "It was my happy duty," he wrote in his autobiography, "to hire hundreds of [the Navajo] as the Indian extras." Ford appreciated Cody's skill as an archer. It was he who rode alongside the coach as it made its dash across the dry lake, "shooting arrows into it and through the windows. We used real arrows for that scene, substituting quick-reflexed stuntmen in the coach for the stars."

According to Ford's grandson Dan, "John's favorite bit player was not a Navajo but an Apache, who had a classic Indian face and lived in a remote canyon far from Monument Valley that was accessible only on horseback. His name was Many Mules and he played Geronimo, the Indian the camera pans to at the start of the chase in *Stagecoach*" (page 164). The film opens with an interrupted message coming over the telegraph wires that contains just a single word: "Geronimo." Ford shrewdly alighted on the Apache rising of the early 1880s, when Geronimo and his braves swept through Arizona, galvanizing the white population and reviving everyone's fascination with the West.

According to Joseph McBride, Ford spent some sixty thousand dollars in the reservation during the filming of *Stagecoach.* He shot a further six features in Monument Valley, concluding with *Cheyenne Autumn,* which cost more than six million dollars and must have brought a sizable revenue to the Navajo community. Since then,

Ford on location for *Stagecoach,* with Navajo

The Indians ready to attack in *Stagecoach*, with the Apache leader Geronimo (played by Many Mules) at right

innumerable TV commercials have helped to sustain the economy of the reservation.

In addition, Ford arranged for the U.S. military to drop supplies into Monument Valley during a particularly harsh winter after *Stagecoach* had been made, so that there would be sufficient food for the Navajo and their flocks. Once he completed *My Darling Clementine*, he donated the entire Western street set to the Navajo—although the buildings had to be dismantled five years later and sold for scrap.

Harry Goulding told Peter Bogdanovich in the 1960s: "[Ford's] been taken into the Navajo tribe, you know. They have a special name for 'im, the Navajos. Natani Nez. That's his name, only his. Natani Nez. It means the Tall Soldier." The "knighting" of Ford occurred during the production of *The Searchers*, on the Fourth of July 1955, when the Navajo presented the director with a scarred deer hide and took him into their number as an honorary Native American.

The Navajo population in and around Monument Valley has grown to 180,000, and they sustain a fragile economy with their flocks of sheep providing just enough wool for a variety of much-coveted rugs. If Goulding remains their favorite white man, then John Ford runs a close second in the memory of many Navajo still alive today, such as Suzie Yazzie, who appears in *The Searchers*, and David Lee Clark, who was seventeen when Ford used him as an extra and assistant in *Cheyenne Autumn*.

That credit sequence in *Stagecoach* does indeed establish much of the imagery that would render Ford's subsequent Westerns so distinctive. Beneath a heavy, brooding layer of clouds, the coach and horses gallop down what the Navajo later dubbed "Hollywood Boulevard"—a dusty stretch of rutted track (below). Next comes the U.S. Cavalry, trotting in escort. Finally, after a dissolve, mounted Indians emerge from the sunset's shadows to add a touch of menace to the scene. Ford actually used the dramatic vistas of Monument Valley rather sparingly in *Stagecoach*, then more amply in *My Darling Clementine, Fort Apache, She Wore a Yellow Ribbon, The Searchers, Sergeant Rutledge,* and *Cheyenne Autumn*. In these later films, Ford's characters dwell in the shadow of mesas and towering buttresses; they often appear puny by comparison with the immutable rock that looms over them (opposite). As J. A. Place has written, "Ford uses [Monument Valley] as Homer used the sea. It is rather like the sea in its changes, its colors, its moods. Like the sea and unlike lush plains or green mountains, it is resistant to human efforts to shape it, to make it serve them."

In *Stagecoach,* Ford depicts with strong, unerring strokes an image of the West as a hostile environment, vast and ungovernable, so intimidating that the stage-

This rough "road" across the desert floor in Monument Valley was dubbed "Hollywood Boulevard" by Navajo helping with the filming of *Stagecoach*. Courtesy of the author

coach must dash across the floor of Monument Valley from one small settlement to another. Once it has left Tonto, the stagecoach scurries across the immense valley floor between Merrick Butte and the Mittens—before the camera wheels left to discover the Indians contemplating attack. Whenever individual monuments, such as El Capitan or Mitchell Butte, figure within a composition in *Stagecoach,* they remain in the background, a discreet reminder of the mythical frontier that divided the civilized world from that of the dark and dangerous "savage." This landscape scarcely resembles the Garden of Eden represented in the paintings of Bierstadt and Moran, and certainly not the lush forests of Hawkeye and Hiawatha. It is a harsh, abrasive desert, bereft of agriculture and thick with Apache (as represented in the film by Navajo).

My Darling Clementine and *Fort Apache* each reserve interiors for some of the most dramatic episodes, but the natural architecture of Monument Valley lends an ominous dimension to many of the location sequences. Distant buttes in *Stagecoach* loom menacingly over the Earp brothers at the start of *My Darling Clementine;* later in the film, however, Mitchell Butte seems to play a more comforting symbolic role during the ceremonial dance at the site of the new church. In *Fort Apache,* the opening shot behind the credits shows a bugler in the eerie shadow of a butte. Colonel Thursday's daughter (Shirley Temple), out riding with her swain (played by John Agar), asks him the name of a distant outcrop. "Blue Mesa," he replies. When she suggests that they go there, he tells her, "It's not as close as it seems," underscoring the great emptiness of the valley.

Indeed, Ford uses the open stretches of the desert floor of Monument Valley more pointedly here than in any other Western. The Apache attack Sergeant Beaufort's repair wagon on the plain south of Square Rock, and the same landscape is used for the meeting at which Colonel Thursday insults and threatens Cochise. The tall fingers of the Totem Pole rock formation seem to be admonishing Captain York and Beaufort as the two ride cautiously over the sand dunes in search of Cochise's encampment. When Thursday's doomed regiment rides out at dawn, the buttes are swathed in mysterious morning clouds.

The climax, shot in Rock Door Canyon (below), just behind the site of Goulding's Lodge, takes advantage of the sand and wind as the Indians massacre Colonel Thursday (based unmistakably on the character of George Armstrong Custer) and his men. Ford shows the soldiers hunkered down at the mouth of the canyon, easy prey for the marauding wave of Apache braves. But their slaughter is observed in long shot, through a scrim of dust kicked up by the horses' hooves.

The entrance to Rock Door Canyon in Monument Valley, where Ford shot the gruesome finale of *Fort Apache*. Courtesy of the author

Captain Brittles (John Wayne) leads his cavalry troop (complete with dog) across Monument Valley in *She Wore a Yellow Ribbon*.

Then Captain York waits with his men on a ridge, in view of Mitchell Butte and the Mittens, for a massive onslaught by the enemy—one that never comes, for Cochise, unlike Colonel Thursday, has sufficient honor not to perpetrate unprovoked further massacre. One almost feels that Ford was reluctant to show the gory truth of the Little Big Horn; the dust of Monument Valley comes to his aid and casts a veil over the ghastly day—helped by cameraman Archie Stout's use of infrared film.

She Wore a Yellow Ribbon (opposite) marks the brightest moment in the Western career of John Ford. The central pillar of his cavalry trilogy, the film works to some degree as a sequel to *Fort Apache,* for the opening narration talks of the death of Custer and the unification of tribes under Sitting Bull and Crazy Horse to resist the white man's invasion. However, although it was made in 1949, only a year after *Fort Apache,* it could hardly be further removed from the earlier film. Perhaps *Fort Apache*'s astringent mood, the misanthropic character of Henry Fonda's Colonel Thursday, and the inexorable slaughter of his men at the hands of the Indians left Ford yearning for light and warmth.

The biggest change is an aesthetic one. Ford used color for the first time in a Western, and he took Winton C. Hoch as his cinematographer. Hoch had experimented with Technicolor at the Walt Disney Studios in the early 1940s, and he had impressed Ford during the shooting of *3 Godfathers* (which hovers between being a Western and a biblical parable) in 1948 (page 172). The same year he had brought a rich palette of colors to Victor Fleming's version of *Joan of Arc*. Now Ford asked him to study the paintings of Frederic Remington. Never one to bestow praise on his crew, save when essential, Ford in his old age claimed the credit for the look of *She Wore a Yellow Ribbon:* "I tried to copy the Remington style—you can't copy him one hundred percent—but at least I tried to get in his color and movement, and I think I succeeded partly." Brian W. Dippie has written of Remington, "Besides mid-day glare and his moonlights and firelights, he painted figures caught in the eerie orange glow of early evening, when shadows are at their longest, just before the sun slips from sight." Remington's wonderfully bright and ocherous

John Wayne, Harry
Carey Jr., and Pedro
Armendariz in
3 Godfathers, Ford's
desert parable

Evening in the Desert, Navajoes, for example, communicates the atmosphere of
desert and mountain range bathed in transfiguring light (opposite).

Suddenly Monument Valley has become a more hospitable environment. The
Indians may still gaze down at the landscape from its higher elevations, while the
cavalry is almost absorbed into the vastness of the valley (page 174), but this
remains a mythical, vivid stretch of terrain (page 175) that Captain Nathan Brittles
clearly regards as home. The cabin where he lives and works is made of a wood that
seems to glow in the sunlight, like the red of the sheer, bauxite Rock Door Mesa
that shelters it (page 176). Such frontier army posts not only protected existing
farms but also became a nucleus for future settlement. Located on the site of
Goulding's Lodge, Brittles's cabin has been preserved as part of a museum devoted

Frederic Remington.
*Evening in the Desert,
Navajoes*. 1905–6. Oil
on canvas, 20 x 26".
Courtesy Frederic
Remington Art Museum,
Ogdensburg, New York

The West Mitten (at right). The fort in *She Wore a Yellow Ribbon* was built near the road in the middle distance. Courtesy Carlo Gaberscek

to Ford and the Westerns shot in Monument Valley. As the filmmaker John Milius has commented, "Ford made Monument Valley the image of the West. . . . He would always get a low angle, low horizon, the wind blowing the grass, if possible to be a lighter color than the sky. These were images no one else could get on film. He was genuinely having a love affair with the land."

Brittles, like Ford himself, is nourished on pathos. He is not disfigured by the racial bigotry of a Colonel Thursday or an Ethan Edwards. He has spent his career not simply in loyal service to the U.S. Cavalry, but also in striving to comprehend the Indian way of life. The eloquent encounter between Brittles and Pony That Walks describes this feeling. Both men suffer from the infirmities and exasperations of old age. Solitude is the price paid by leaders such as Brittles and Thursday—but Brittles, unlike Thursday, does not sacrifice moral integrity.

Nathan Brittles's cabin in *She Wore a Yellow Ribbon,* constructed—and still standing—at Goulding's Lodge, Monument Valley. Courtesy Carlo Gaberscek

When he talks to his long-dead wife at her grave, Brittles says he's thinking of going farther west, to California maybe, rather than retiring to his midwestern roots on the banks of the Wabash. The nostalgia that courses through the film concerns Brittles alone, however; Ford does not mourn some paradise lost in the mists of the antebellum Southwest or the Far West prior to the massacre at the Little Big Horn. Nevertheless, J. A. Place argues, "The greatest force in *She Wore a Yellow Ribbon* is the past, rooted in American mythology. That Ford places the American dream in the past instead of in its usual position in the future of his characters' lives is an indication of his growing disillusionment with that dream and his realization of its unreality."

Death in the field comes regularly to Ford's characters, whether it be James Earp in *My Darling Clementine* or the former Confederate brigadier general known as "Trooper" Smith in *She Wore a Yellow Ribbon*. Their burials signify a return to the earth, and their graves in Monument Valley are as hallowed as any pharaoh's.

Evocations of Remington (below)—and Russell—may be found in the shots of a single rider waving against the skyline, and in the wild and storm-riven skies during the march to Sudrose Wells. (This desert storm must have been as capricious and fortunate an occurrence for Ford as was the snowfall during the filming of *Stagecoach*.) The vast outdoors location is plunged into semidarkness, resulting in imagery of a strange and haunting allure. The parallels with Remington should not be stretched too far, however, for the artist painted cowboys more than soldiers.

Although *Rio Grande* and *Wagon Master* both make rich use of desert locations, neither 1950 film belongs to Ford's Monument Valley canon. He would have liked

Frederic Remington. *The Quest.* 1901. Oil on canvas, 27⁷⁄₁₆ x 40³⁄₈". Courtesy of The Anschutz Collection, Denver, Colorado

to shoot *Rio Grande* in the valley for the sake of consistency with the first two pictures in the cavalry trilogy, but after a battle with his producer that left him "a nervous wreck," he opted for Moab, Utah, as he did with *Wagon Master*. In fact, White's Ranch and Castle Valley contain buttes almost identical to those in Monument Valley, so that the fort in *Rio Grande* looks much the same as it does in *Fort Apache,* although the light seems brighter and more optimistic. The texture of rock, as well as the almost prehistoric relief enveloping Professor Valley, matches Monument Valley almost perfectly.

Ford returned to Monument Valley in 1955 for the shooting of *The Searchers* (opposite); the film depends in huge measure on its rock formations, using them to advance the plot and serve as metaphors for an implacable odyssey (page 180). Homer would have loved the petrified majesty of Monument Valley. One cannot imagine a more rugged cradle for myth.

Right in the opening shot, as Martha Edwards advances through the doorway to confront the desert beyond, one sees Mitchell Butte and Gray Whiskers, colossal guardians of the valley (page 181, top). Even the dense "snakewood" bush works to Ford's advantage, as Martha gazes out into the dusk and sees the flash and glint of Comanche signals. Gradually the buttes and towers play their role in the long search for the Indians' captives. The West (or Left) Mitten, seen behind Ethan as he observes the burning farm and also featured during the burial service for the Edwards family, can be argued to represent a mother and child, underscoring the kinship theme in *The Searchers*. A dead bull is found near the North Window (see page 185), framing a spectacular horizon. Huge, planed boulders form a makeshift grave for one of the Comanche braves who attacked the Edwards household (page 181, bottom). A daunting cleft between two massive rock formations conceals the mutilated corpse of young Lucy (although Ford, with characteristic restraint, leaves the gruesome details to the imagination). The intimidating north side of Square Rock adds to the baleful sight of the Indians preparing to attack the Reverend Captain Clayton and his Texas Rangers. In a later sequence, Clayton and Ethan

Poster for *The Searchers*, emphasizing the skies above Monument Valley

John Wayne as Ethan Edwards looks down at the Comanche encampment in *The Searchers*, as Monument Valley endows the shot with an eerie sense of vertigo.

Gray Whiskers and Mitchell Butte as they may be seen at the start of *The Searchers*. Courtesy Carlo Gaberscek

The heavy boulders that mark the spot where the body of a Comanche brave is uncovered by Ethan Edwards and his companions in *The Searchers*. Courtesy of the author

survey the Comanche camp from what locals have dubbed "John Ford Point"—a slender promontory of rock overlooking a spectacular stretch of Monument Valley (above). The so-called Totem Pole formation (see page 195), fronted by sand dunes, offers a noble backdrop to the scene of Ethan being led by his Mexican informant to the Comanche camp. "John Ford Point" is again used to show Martin Pawley being lowered silently by night to the valley floor so that he can enter the Comanche camp undetected.

Pursued by Scar's braves, Ethan and Martin flee to the sanctuary of a narrow, arch-shaped cave, and Ford uses its unusual configuration from within and without. In the penultimate sequence of the film, Debbie, believing that Ethan is about to kill her, also rushes up to the mouth of the grotto. Today, visitors will find that

"John Ford Point" as it is today. Courtesy Carlo Gaberscek

spot jammed with discarded trash and machinery from a Navajo settlement close by (below).

During the shooting of *She Wore a Yellow Ribbon,* Ford had grown fond of a stretch of the San Juan River in Utah, near Mexican Hat, some twenty-five miles northeast of Monument Valley (page 184, top). This explains the abrupt, rather jarring—even, by Ford's standards, clumsy—transition in *The Searchers* from the Rangers galloping ahead of the pursuing Comanche in Monument Valley to their splashing into the turbid waters of the San Juan. The ridged terraces of russet rock and sienna sand that rise up from the riverbank are, however, sufficiently close in texture to those of the nearby Monument Valley for the locations to match smoothly (page 184, bottom).

Joseph McBride believes that Ford's instinctive sensitivity for landscape stems from his youth: "Commuting through the Irish countryside for a few weeks while attending a school near his ancestral home, John became fully aware of the pictorial splendor of landscape and its connections with the lives of ordinary people. As

The cave mouth where Ethan Edwards (John Wayne) and Martin Pawley (Jeffrey Hunter) take shelter from the Comanche in *The Searchers*. Today, the Navajo use it as a dumping ground for domestic hardware. Courtesy of the author

The San Juan River at Mexican Hat, Utah, the location Ford used for the scenes of fighting with the Indians in both *The Searchers* and *Sergeant Rutledge*. Courtesy Carlo Gaberscek

The San Juan River, which the characters played by Ward Bond, John Wayne, and their companions cross in *The Searchers*. Courtesy Carlo Gaberscek

The North Window is featured as a location in *The Searchers* and again in *Sergeant Rutledge*. Courtesy Carlo Gaberscek

Orson Welles once said of him, 'John Ford knows what the earth is made of.'" Only Ford could have realized the most mysterious image in the entire film: a high long shot of Ethan and Martin traversing the floor of Monument Valley, with a gigantic cloud of dust to their left, and the landscape seemingly alive with light and texture.

Ford spent nine days on location in Monument Valley for *Sergeant Rutledge*. Two casual references to the "Jorgensen ranch" serve as reminders of *The Searchers,* which used similar locations. "Spindle Station," where the hapless young Mary Beecher must spend an anxious night in the company of the wounded sergeant, affords a spectacular view over the valley identical to that from Goulding's Lodge. The North Window (above) serves as a backdrop for the scene in which Chris Hubble, the sutler's son, is found staked out in the broiling sun. Other monuments glimpsed in the film include the Three Sisters and the Totem Pole, as well as Mexican Hat outside the valley, which is seen looming behind Rutledge as he watches the Apache attack the ranch at Spanish Wells.

"My Favorite Location"

Ford gave Harry Goulding scant credit for introducing him to this spectacular location. Asked by Peter Bogdanovich a quarter of a century later how he had found Monument Valley, the director responded curtly, "I had traveled up there once, driving through Arizona on my way to Santa Fe, New Mexico." As early as 1919, Ford had ventured into the charming Rio Grande Valley to make *Ace of the Saddle*. But once he found this new spot, he kept going back. "My favorite location is Monument Valley," confirmed Ford. "It has rivers, mountains, plains, desert, everything the land can offer. I feel at peace there. I have been all over the world, but I consider this the most complete, beautiful, and peaceful place on earth."

Most Westerns had been shot in terrain close to the coast, within easy reach of Hollywood. During the 1930s, Gallup, New Mexico, became a center for Western production, with stars staying at the picturesque El Rancho inn. George O'Brien, who had starred in early Ford Westerns, worked on some productions during the 1930s in Kayenta, Arizona, outside Monument Valley. But the valley itself must have seemed impossibly remote in the days before air travel. In 1938, Harry Goulding was painfully aware that his beloved valley was farther away from a railroad line than any other location in the continental United States—some 180 miles. The region was bereft not just of proper roads and bridges, but even of telephones. Once filming started there, supplies from Hollywood needed to be routed via Flagstaff and trundled into the valley along rutted tracks. Iron Eyes Cody, who worked with Ford on *Stagecoach,* recalled, "We had to lay plank-boards over the dirt paths and sand, which the trucks had to follow carefully, or sink."

Even today, the thirty-mile-long Monument Valley remains about a six-hour drive from Santa Fe to the southeast, eight hours from Denver to the northeast, and eight hours from Las Vegas to the west; the Grand Canyon, seemingly not far to the west, is about three hours away by car. Perhaps Ford relished the thought of such isolation—a place where front-office executives could not exasperate him with their bureaucratic demands. He and the principal actors in *Stagecoach* stayed at the Wetherills' inn and trading post beyond the southern end of Monument Valley, in Kayenta. Twenty-six crew members camped at the Gouldings' trading post, where water and food were literally the only facilities available. A clear image of Goulding's Lodge as it was in the 1940s may be seen early in *Fort Apache,* when Colonel Owen Thursday arrives at just such a trading post and is offered a drink by the Scottish proprietress.

The statistics of Monument Valley explain why horsemen and houses alike look so diminutive in its midst. It lies more than fifty-two hundred feet above sea level, and the majority of its buttes, arches, towers, and mesas soar abruptly a further thousand feet toward the

Stagecoach: John Ford on location in Monument Valley with Tim Holt. © 1978 Ned Scott Archive/MPTV.net

Stagecoach: The two Mittens dominate the left and center of the composition, giving it a stereoscopic quality. © 1978 Ned Scott Archive/MPTV.net

inescapable sun. Monument Valley comprises more than four hundred square miles. The escarpments as well as the desert floor seem to smolder with the pinkish red of iron bauxite. Yet the landscape is by no means barren. Yucca and black sage, juniper, tamarisk, and cottonwood trees emerge from the dusty, rocky soil.

In prehistoric times, the area was in a state of volcanic upheaval. Mountains reared up and then were folded by prodigious forces of nature, falling back into the hammada (rock-strewn desert). Gigantic tubes of molten lava relapsed everywhere, congealing, sliver by sliver, chunk by chunk, into what had been in effect a salt seabed. Since then, ferocious winds and relentless storms have pared, planed, striated, and sliced the surviving cores of De Chelly sandstone, leaving them to rear with uncanny smoothness into the firmament. Monuments such as El Capitan (seen early on in *Stagecoach*) are all that remain of the spouting lava after it hardened and its outer carapace of softer material was abraded by the elements. At the feet of each butte or spire lies a tumble of boulders, as if scooped from the parent rock and flung aside. As Andrew Sinclair has written, "the gigantic sculptures of time and weather . . . make the efforts of mankind appear irrelevant and vain." It is easy, of course, to accept the scientific explanations. Yet if one stands in the lee of a mighty butte and gazes up its beveled, gleaming flank toward the heavens, it is hard not to accord some respect to the Navajo belief that Monument Valley was created by the gods.

Everywhere one looks, space appears foreshortened (opposite). A sign indicates that the Visitor Center is a full four miles away, but to the naked eye the buildings seem no more than a few hundred yards up the road. To all intents and purposes, Monument Valley has not changed since the first day John Ford came upon it.

"A legend is more interesting than the actual facts," said John Ford in a taped interview not long before his death. Two years after *Sergeant Rutledge,* he explored the contrast between the legend and fact in his next-to-last feature-length Western, *The Man Who Shot Liberty Valance* (1962). For this very different kind of Ford Western, the director abandoned Monument Valley. The result is by no means visually inspiring. It is a garrulous, occasionally boring Western that takes place almost entirely indoors, with Ford returning to his favorite format of black-and-white. But as J. A. Place has observed, "the film's visual style lacks more than light: the effect of the darkness is to reduce the mythical proportions of the film, to confine the story within the boundaries of legend rather than to expand it, as the beautiful photography of *My Darling Clementine* does." As dry as a martini, this disquisition on history and its distortions nonetheless has a redeeming humor, as well as the rare sight of John Wayne and James Stewart appearing in the same story.

Ford often said it was the folklore of the Old West that intrigued him. A mood of wistfulness invades every exchange of dialogue in *The Man Who Shot Liberty Valance.* When Vera Miles's Hallie Stoddard returns to town after a long absence, she laments the way everything has changed, to which the old former marshal replies, "The desert's still the same." Yet Hallie comments to Stewart's Ransom Stoddard, "If they ever dam the river we'll have lots of water—and lots of different flowers." The stagecoach has given way to the train, and the continent has dramatically shrunk. The train manager who, like everyone else, believes that Senator Stoddard indeed is "the man who shot Liberty Valance"—the foundation of Stoddard's long and distinguished career—assures him that he will catch the express and be back in Washington, D.C., in two days and nights, a fraction of the time it took such courageous Easterners as Mrs. Mallory in *Stagecoach* or Miss Carter in *My Darling Clementine.*

The average age of Ford's characters increased over the years, as he began to identify more intimately with the roles played by actors such as Wayne and Stewart. In a changing world, the characters became—almost imperceptibly—obsolescent.

Buddy Roosevelt, who appears uncredited and anonymous here, was a veteran once featured as "Buddy" in a whole series of Westerns during the 1920s. Stewart's marshal in *Two Rode Together* at least had some fire in his corrupt belly, but in *The Man Who Shot Liberty Valance,* Andy Devine's upholder of the law in Shinbone is both plump and spineless, even less commendable than his Sergeant Posey in *Two Rode Together*. Ford has begun to accept that this may have been the reality of the Old West, a place where marksmen were scarce and most people fell victim to a random bullet. Even Lee Marvin's gunfighter Valance becomes a parody of characters such as Jack Palance's hired killer in George Stevens's *Shane,* as well as a persona—"Liberty Palance," perhaps—that Marvin would adapt to uproarious heights in *Cat Ballou* three years later.

Ford released *Liberty Valance* in 1962, at a juncture in American history that did not yet relish either satire or the lampooning of history. President John F. Kennedy was stirring the youth of the world with grandiloquent rhetoric. Meanwhile, the French New Wave and similar movements in Great Britain, Italy, and Eastern Europe made Ford's technique appear lumbering and irredeemably outmoded.

Who, one might ask, in fact cares about history, apart from those who are themselves part of it? In *The Man Who Shot Liberty Valance,* Edmond O'Brien's unforgettable Dutton Peabody, "founder, owner, publisher, and editor" of the *Shinbone Star,* tries valiantly to attach some credit to the Fourth Estate; he flounders about in a drunken stupor but finally spurs the territory's voters to send Stoddard to Washington as their representative. Peabody's successor as editor, Maxwell Scott (Carleton Young), cuts an altogether more urbane figure. It is he who declares to the much older Senator Stoddard, after hearing the true story of his life in Shinbone: "This is the West, sir. When the legend becomes fact, print the legend." In many respects, Ford did that throughout his entire career, even in quasi-historical films such as *Mary of Scotland* and *The Prisoner of Shark Island*.

Yet even when Ford exposes the fact behind the legend, he does not explode the myths that he himself has helped to create. He declines to mock the setting of Monument Valley, for example, or the fundamental idea that the "Western" man was essentially a slave to his environment, at the mercy of the elements, the deserts and mountains, and Native Americans who understandably fought to preserve their sacred hunting grounds. Nor, in *Liberty Valance,* does he scorn the concept of family loyalty that underpins his classic work.

For Joseph McBride, Ford's biographer and a passionate fan of the film, "the almost total *absence* of landscape from *Liberty Valance* is itself a statement of Ford's loss of faith in the ideal of the American frontier; the civilization of Shinbone seems a dead end." However, contemporary critics excoriated the film for its artifice and drabness of look. Manny Farber, for example, described its setting as "an unreal

The aftermath of the gunfight in *The Man Who Shot Liberty Valance*

stage town . . . where the cactus was planted last night." Bosley Crowther in the *New York Times* found it synthetic, "an almost slapdash entertainment that is a bit of a baffling oddity."

Ford decided to shoot in black-and-white not for budgetary reasons, but because he felt that the gunfight involving Valance, Stoddard, and a concealed Tom Doniphon (Wayne) needed subtle variations of shadow and light (opposite). One senses that perhaps he yearned to return to his early days, filming Westerns quickly and cheaply with Harry Carey Sr. *The Man Who Shot Liberty Valance* actually delights in its contrived quality. The Western genre has been around so long, Ford seems to be saying, that it should be debunked as much as history itself. In that sense, it opened the way for a variety of other satirical works, from *Cat Ballou* to *Paint Your Wagon* and *Blazing Saddles*. In a more somber register, Clint Eastwood's *Unforgiven* also owes something to *Liberty Valance*.

The characters played by Wayne and Stewart in *Liberty Valance* embody the opposing poles of opinion concerning the Far West. Tom Doniphon believes in the gun as a means of staying alive. "Out here, a man settles his own problems," he tells Stoddard, the young, idealistic lawyer from the East. Like most gunfighters, Doniphon turns to liquor when the tension rises, letting the rage well up within him to a point at which he sets fire to his own home. Liberty Valance himself takes several pulls at the bottle before lurching out for his final showdown with Stoddard. The editor Peabody moves in a constant state of intoxication, taking a quick nip (shielding the bottle with his hat) before delivering the most ironic and eloquent speech in the film. He recalls "the vast herd of buffalo and savage redskin roaming our beautiful territory . . . and then, with the westward march of our nation came the pioneer and the buffalo hunter, the adventurous and the bold. And the boldest of these were the cattlemen, who seized the wide open range for their own personal domain—and their law was the law of the hired gun. . . . But now we need statehood to protect the rights of every man and woman, however humble." Even Doc Willoughby (Ken Murray) gulps down some whiskey before daring to pronounce Valance well and truly dead. The only character to refuse a dram is Doniphon's black hired hand, Pompey (Woody Strode), who rescues his employer and shows more integrity than any white man in the movie.

As the train leaves Shinbone at the end, and Stoddard muses that he should quit his duties in Washington and return to set up a law office in the town that made him famous, Hallie gazes out the window. "It was once a wilderness; now it's a garden," she says, in ironic refutation of the mid-nineteenth-century vision of that earlier West as an unspoiled Garden of Eden. Ford, one feels, is in some degree questioning the contribution of railroads, dams, schools. His heart hankers after an unadulterated West, as immutable as the roseate buttes of Monument Valley, nowhere in sight here. In Ed Buscombe's happy dictum, "Ford humanizes history."

In terms of visual splendor, Ford waited until he was in his late sixties and directing his final Western, *Cheyenne Autumn,* to present Monument Valley in its full glory. The immensity of the 70mm (Super Panavision) image releases the majestic proportions of the area from the confines of the old, squarer, so-called Academy format. Each monument gives off a specific resonance; each seems like a physical component of Native American life and beliefs. As Dolores Del Rio's Spanish Woman and Sal Mineo's Red Shirt emerge from their tepee, the Totem Pole stelae rise up behind them, eloquent testimonial to the Native Americans' place in the terrain (opposite). Ford underlines the indissoluble bond that exists between the Cheyenne and their environment as he shows the dead chief being buried beneath rocks and then sealed into this natural tomb, recalling the scene in *The Searchers* when the corpse of a Comanche brave is discovered beneath the boulders.

Ford dwells on aspects of Monument Valley that he had not had time to relish in earlier films: the sensuous undulation of the dunes; the clumps of tenacious prairie grass punctuating the desert floor; the tactile quality of the sand, which spills away from the Cheyenne women as they dig trenches for protection; the smooth, slender rocks that surge up in line as though forming the sides of a ruined abbey. And William Clothier's camera brings out the fundamental ocher of the land, with autumn leaves as yellow as the sand, the sun, and the cavalry kerchiefs.

Although the real Cheyenne were held on reservations in Oklahoma, Ford integrates them into the topography of Arizona's Monument Valley to excellent metaphorical effect. He takes poetic license by repeating shots of certain rock

Cheyenne Autumn: The Cheyenne survey the Totem Pole formation in Monument Valley.

formations, paying a price in terms of narrative pace but emphasizing the Native Americans' accord with their surroundings. However fast or slow they march, the Cheyenne's trek through the brutal winter cold of Nebraska leads them not to the "green and fertile" territory of Wyoming some fifteen hundred miles to the north, but endlessly back to the buttes and mesas of Monument Valley. Their final refuge is Victory Cave, supposedly in the mountains of Dakota Territory—but it is in fact the same cleft in the rocks in which Ethan and Martin took shelter in *The Searchers*. So, forty-seven years after making his first Western, Ford brought to a close his devotion to the genre. Monument Valley has become a location that bears witness to Ford's distortion of history as well as his unimpeachable humanity.

Frederic Remington.
In from the Night Herd.
1907. Oil on canvas,
27 x 40". National
Cowboy & Western
Heritage Museum,
Oklahoma City,
Oklahoma 75.19.2C.3

CHAPTER 6

THE TELLTALE SIGNATURE

Ford's signature can be found, like that of any great painter or composer, throughout his major works.

When, for example, Martin Pawley first appears in *The Searchers,* he is seen riding up to the door of the homestead and leaping off in an elegant gesture—almost exactly the same shot as in Ford's first feature, *Straight Shooting,* some forty years earlier, when Hoot Gibson dismounts in front of a doorway. Ford's fondness for the "Ann Rutledge theme," first used in *Young Mr. Lincoln,* means that it can also be heard at fitting moments in Westerns such as *The Searchers* and *The Horse Soldiers.* His frequent introduction of rousing folk songs or traditional melodies enlivens the narrative and serves as an offscreen kind of chorus to comment on the action. Gilbert Adair has observed, "Ford's use of campfire songs to punctuate his plot-lines echoes Kipling's fondness for Cockney, aitch-dropping barrack-room ballads as chapter-heads."

Like Shakespeare, Ford sought to leaven his dramatic tales with moments of light relief: the court scenes involving Judge Haller and the knockabout comedy involving the removal of Casey's tooth, both in *The Iron Horse;* the Granville Thorndyke scenes in *My Darling Clementine;* the court-martial shenanigans in *Sergeant Rutledge;* and the Dodge City sequence in *Cheyenne Autumn,* to cite but a few examples.

Ford himself was not John Wayne, not Henry Fonda, not even James Stewart, but rather the character actor Hank Worden, when as Mose Harper he relaxes in his rocking chair on the porch of the Jorgensens' house near the end of *The Searchers,* smiling happily at the safe return of Debbie. As Ford said on one occasion, he enjoyed finding "the extraordinary in the ordinary, and heroism in the everyday."

Yet for all his family instincts, the essential solitude of the frontiersman appealed to Ford as well. Whether it be a bareheaded John Wayne standing tall against the twilit sky in *Rio Grande,* or Ben Johnson waving his cap back to his troop from a red rock high above the river in *She Wore a Yellow Ribbon,* Ford's choice of low camera angle insists on the heroic dimension of the shot. Ford also gave the interior scenes in *Stagecoach* a claustrophobic perspective, by using a similar angle and ceilinged sets—a full two years before Orson Welles and Gregg Toland did the same in *Citizen Kane.*

Andrew Sinclair has noted Ford's inspired use of bad weather, in this instance during the shooting of *Fort Apache.* Rain started to fall as the seven hundred Mormon extras playing the U.S. Cavalry were getting into position to jog down the hill into Monument Valley. Henry Fonda told Sinclair: "It's one of the all-time great shots. I mean, you could see the moisture on the leather. It had a little glisten to it. It had a quality, a feeling, it wouldn't have had with the sun. Now he didn't know it was going to happen like that. It happened and he used it. And it's so right." When Hoot Gibson's horse stumbled while crossing a river in *Straight Shooting,* Joseph McBride reminds us, Ford kept the camera going as the star remounted and continued across the river. There's much the same sense of spontaneity in *The Searchers* when Ward Bond's mount flounders in the frantic fording of the San Juan River, with the Comanche in pursuit.

Before embarking on *The Searchers,* Ford went into a hospital for the removal of cataracts. Impatient, he took off the bandage on one eye too early, thus depriving it of sight completely. McBride contends that "Ford's tendency toward bolder visual brush strokes in his later films and his diminishing interest in minute detail work can be attributed in part to his poor eyesight." In *Sergeant Rutledge,* he did not flinch from using black as a predominant color in several scenes, shutting down the light in the courtroom until Constance Towers is a silhouette. The darkness becomes her innermost being, her subconscious. Ford crafts a similar impression at the start of *The Searchers,* as Martha Edwards "emerges" from her innermost thoughts to confront the bright reality of the desert and the approaching figure of Ethan, the man she has loved in vain. Shadows conceal other dangers in the campfire sequences in both *The Searchers* and *Two Rode Together,* as Ethan

Edwards and Guthrie McCabe respectively keep their eyes alert for ambush. Frederic Remington's *In from the Night Herd* (page 196) also captures the latent fear and isolation of such scenes.

Ford's approach to life could never be accused of detachment. His faults as a filmmaker include tendencies toward sentimentality, levity, and bitterness. As Welles has said, "Sentiment is Jack's vice. When he escapes it, you get a perfect kind of innocence. *Young Mr. Lincoln,* for instance. How truly great that is! And what a sense he always has for texture—for the physical existence of things."

Ford's characters could be as curmudgeonly on screen as he himself was in life. He found it difficult to deal with any passion or serious romance between the sexes. His guilt as a gruff and often absentee father in private life worked its way

Father and son: John Wayne (right) and Claude Jarman Jr. in *Rio Grande*

into the complex relationship between Captain York and his son, Jeff, in *Rio Grande* (opposite). Yet Jeff's courage under fire, as well as the bravery of the children in that film, underlines Ford's belief in the future, and the obligation to pass the torch from one generation to the next.

Ford's patriotism often reached unsustainable levels, and it led him to a naïve admiration for all things military. His optimism might have made even Rousseau blush, although on many occasions his humanism came to the rescue of a hackneyed plot. Despite the cynicism of *The Man Who Shot Liberty Valance* and *Cheyenne Autumn,* he presented a West in which whites rarely succumb to brutality (though one should not forget Jesson's betrayal of Davy in *The Iron Horse,* as he cuts the rope above the pass). He could never have made a film as cruel as *Nevada Smith,* nor any of the Anthony Mann Westerns of the 1950s (even if *Bend of the River* has a Fordian ring to it). The miners and prospectors are far more convincing in Mann's *The Far Country* than they are in *My Darling Clementine*. Ford was a man of the desert, not, like Mann, of the high, unforgiving mountains and the snows. His most redeeming feature remains his poetic instinct for placing men and horses in the vast expanse of Monument Valley.

Of course, his Westerns do contain moments of violence, all the more startling for their abruptness and unpredictability. One thinks of the young Clegg being viciously horsewhipped on a wagon wheel after raping an Indian woman in *Wagon Master*. Or Old Man Clanton lashing his sons with his whip after Wyatt Earp has humiliated them in *My Darling Clementine*. Or Ethan Edwards in *The Searchers,* swooping into Scar's tepee to take his scalp.

Spurned on its first release, accused of being too long, too ponderous, and too superficial in its rehabilitation of the Native American, *Cheyenne Autumn* (pages 202, 203) has found recognition among a new generation, especially in France, where its rerelease in 2003 was greeted with two full pages of analysis in the newspaper *Libération*. What contemporary critics failed to see in 1964 was that Ford's final Western actually heralded a new idiom for the genre, one in which psychology and inner feelings would replace the thunder of hooves and the clash of arms. Sam

Dolores Del Rio in
Cheyenne Autumn

OPPOSITE
Chief Dan George made
a small, uncredited
appearance in
Cheyenne Autumn.

Peckinpah, Robert Aldrich, Sergio Leone, and Clint Eastwood have all directed Westerns that owe something to the brooding, elegiac atmosphere of *Cheyenne Autumn.*

Remington's control of light beguiled others besides Ford, including Howard Hawks, who sought to capture that light in a single scene outside a saloon. The credit sequences for Robert Parrish's *The Last Hunt* (1955) and William A. Fraker's *Monte Walsh* (1970) feature reproductions of paintings by both Remington and Russell. Ford, however, looked to Remington for inspiration primarily where color was concerned (although he apparently first imitated the artist in *Hell Bent,* a Western made in 1918). The gray murk of an approaching storm in *Stagecoach* is reminiscent of the artist. Remington's *Among the Led Horses* fused two of his favorite hues: a pale blue, mottled with harmless clouds, and an amiable saffron yellow in which the animals revel (below). Cinematographer Winton C. Hoch, who

Frederic Remington. *Among the Led Horses.* 1909. Oil on canvas, 27 x 40". Courtesy Sid Richardson Collection of Western Art, Fort Worth, Texas

won an Academy Award for *She Wore a Yellow Ribbon,* recalled that Ford gave him the laconic brief prior to shooting: "I want Remington color." In the wild, heaving skies en route to Sudrose Wells, the clouds press down toward the floor of Monument Valley as Captain Nathan Brittles leads his troop like a cortege. While the lightning flashes and thunder rolls, the doctor removes a bullet from Corporal Quayne's chest, and the single wagon trundles along as though it were an ark.

In *The Searchers,* as Michael F. Blake has noted, Ford uses color and light to signify emotion, "such as bathing the sky outside the Edwards cabin in an eerie crimson glow, just prior to Scar's attack, suggesting the approaching bloodshed." So Remington, in his *Apache Medicine Song* (below), creates a spectral light emanating from the campfire that recalls the seventeenth-century French artist Georges de La

Frederic Remington. *Apache Medicine Song.* 1908. Oil on canvas, 27⅛ x 29⅞". Courtesy Sid Richardson Collection of Western Art, Fort Worth, Texas

Tour, and that also may have influenced the menacing moments in many a Ford Western, from *She Wore a Yellow Ribbon* to *Two Rode Together*.

The sheer velocity of Ford's tracking shots in *Stagecoach* and other Westerns serves as a cinematic means of mustering action within the frame, just as Remington does in a composition such as *Buffalo Runners—Big Horn Basin* (above). Remington admired the black troopers of the U.S. Cavalry, dubbed Buffalo Soldiers, and Ford's film *Sergeant Rutledge* drew its inspiration from one of the

Frederic Remington. *Buffalo Runners—Big Horn Basin*. 1909. Oil on canvas, 30⅜ x 51½". Courtesy Sid Richardson Collection of Western Art, Fort Worth, Texas

artist's paintings of black soldiers on the western frontier. In *The Alert* (page 208), Remington accentuates the trooper's proud bearing by isolating his upper body against an azure sky and having his head cocked to one side, his gauntleted hand held ready, responsive to the slightest sight and sound that might come across the open desert. Henry Fonda's posture in *My Darling Clementine* resembles that of Remington's rider (page 209).

Hawks declared that Ford had "the greatest vision for a tableau, a long-shot, of any man" (page 210). Eastwood recalled that Leone was "always talking about Ford" and shot *Once Upon a Time in the West* in Monument Valley as a tribute to the Ford tradition. *The Searchers* in particular proved an iconic film for the 1970s generation, including Steven Spielberg, Martin Scorsese, and George Lucas. Eastwood's own *The Outlaw Josey Wales* is imbued with much the same ironic reflections on unjustified celebrity as *The Man Who Shot Liberty Valance*.

Ford's influence extended to the Far East and Akira Kurosawa, whose *Seven Samurai,* with its thundering hooves, recalls the sight and sound of many a Western pursuit, and whose *Yojimbo* gives Toshiro Mifune the role of a silent, heroic individual of the kind that Ford accorded to Wayne and Fonda.

Why is it that a youngster will still embrace classic Westerns like *Red River, Shane* or even *The Magnificent Seven* with such fervor while being perplexed by a fashionable, realistic, revisionist drama such as Clint Eastwood's *Unforgiven*? The more the Western genre sought to penetrate the psychological makeup of its characters, the more it retreated from its outdoor origins, and the less convincing the marriage of man and landscape became. Ford's greatest Westerns, however, show his pioneering families dwarfed by nature, dwelling in simple homesteads at the mercy of Indians and elements alike, in the tradition of pictorial artists such as Albert Bierstadt and Thomas Moran. Laconic actors such as Wayne and Fonda needed few words to express inchoate themes—the odyssey, or reconciliation between old and young, among others—that flowed from the vast open spaces of desert and rock.

Frederic Remington.
The Alert. 1888. Oil on
canvas, 22 x 19½".
Courtesy Frederic
Remington Art Museum,
Ogdensburg, New York

OPPOSITE
Henry Fonda in *My Darling Clementine*,
with the two Mittens in
the background

The thin blue line of cavalry traversing the horizon in *The Horse Soldiers:* an image characteristic of Ford but also of many Western painters

Ford's Westerns differ sharply from most other classics of the genre. They combine a variety of elements that offset one another in a delicate balance. For example, the asperity of *The Searchers* is undermined by the verbal jousting between Martin Pawley and Laurie Jorgensen. The sentimentality of *Rio Grande* is kept in check by the reminders of John Wayne's callous pursuit of duty in setting fire to his wife's estates during the Civil War. The quintessential Ford character is a creature of circumstance, shaped by his environment, susceptible to life's temptations, while retaining an innate dignity and simplicity of purpose.

Through film, and by drawing on his received inspiration from popular literature and his own ingrained patriotism, Ford gave birth to a world in which the sound of the fife and the drum and the rumbling hooves of the U.S. Cavalry inspired not dread but deliverance. Ford's vision stemmed from, and built upon, the late-nineteenth-century images of the West as depicted by Remington, Russell, and Schreyvogel. His work may be described as Remington's was, as "the heartbeat of Western myth." And while one can shrink in horror at the near-extermination of the Native American tribes, one can also, when the lights go down and film or tape or DVD begins to spin, give in to the fables that John Ford—with such simplicity—created.

This silhouette shot
from *Cheyenne Autumn*
evokes some of
Remington's paintings
and bronzes.

OPPOSITE
Ford's use of pale sun-
shine yellow and sunset
red in *The Searchers*
recalls the paintings of
Frederic Remington.

Notes

INTRODUCTION

7   *My name's John Ford* . . . Lindsay Anderson, *About John Ford* (London: Plexus Publishing, 1999).

8   *appealed to me—being about simple people* . . . Joseph McBride, *Searching for John Ford: A Life* (New York: St. Martin's Press, 2001).

9   *The old masters* . . . Ibid.

1. THE MYTH OF THE WEST

13   *The Far West is not America* . . . Philippe Fraisse, "Le Far West: Un imaginaire à la mésure du réel," special Western issue, *Positif,* nos. 509–10 (July–August 2003).
      One of the most striking phases . . . Frederick Jackson Turner, *The Frontier in American History* (New York: Dover Publications, 1996).

14   *The forested region of [the Midwest]* . . . Ibid.
      hardly more than entered . . . Ibid.
      I should point out . . . Iron Eyes Cody, as told to Collin Perry, *Iron Eyes: My Life as a Hollywood Indian* (New York: Everest House, 1982).

15   *Long before the days of '49* . . . Henry Nash Smith, *Virgin Land: The American West as Symbol and Myth* (Cambridge, MA: Harvard University Press, 1950).
      a dreamily beautiful wilderness . . . Ibid.
      delighted in the thought . . . Ibid.
      and ever I am leaving the city . . . Ibid.
      the existence of an uninhabitable desert . . . Ibid.

16   *the Great American Desert* . . . Ibid.
      This hardy band . . . Ibid.
      The wagons, some fifty in number . . . Francis Parkman, *The Oregon Trail* (New York: George P. Putnam, 1849).

17   *home to us the terrible reality* . . . *New York Times,* quoted at http://memory.loc.gov/ammem/cwphtml/cwbrady.htm.
      The conquest and settlement of the West . . . Brian W. Dippie, *The Frederic Remington Art Museum Collection* (New York: Harry N. Abrams, in association with the Frederic Remington Art Museum, 2001).

18   *It looks as if it was painted in an Eldorado* . . . Andrew Wilton and Tim Barringer, eds., *American Sublime: Landscape Painting in the United States, 1820–1880,* exhibition catalogue (London: Tate Publishing, 2002).

20   *I place no value upon literal transcripts* . . . Ed Buscombe, ed., *The BFI Companion to the Western* (London: André Deutsch / BFI Publishing, 1988).

22   *Moran evokes parallels* . . . Wilton and Barringer, *American Sublime.*
      I am working for big effects . . . Dippie, *The Frederic Remington Art Museum Collection.*

23   *I knew the wild riders* . . . Ibid.
      a very recognizable iconography . . . Buscombe, *The BFI Companion to the Western.*

27   *Ford learned the paradoxical method* . . . McBride, *Searching for John Ford.*
      faery land forlorn . . . paraphrase of John Keats, *Ode to a Nightingale* ("Charmed magic casements, opening on the foam / Of perilous seas, in faery lands forlorn").

31   *the myth of the West* . . . Dippie, *The Frederic Remington Art Museum Collection.*
      He pored over it . . . McBride, *Searching for John Ford.*

33   *one of America's strange heroes* . . . Smith, *Virgin Land.*
      In spite of his rude, gross nature . . . Turner, *The Frontier in American History.*

35   *a reality of his own* . . . Dippie, *The Frederic Remington Art Museum Collection.*

2. HISTORY TRANSFIGURED

38   *He told me stories about it* . . . Kevin Brownlow, *The War, the West, and the Wilderness* (New York: Alfred A. Knopf, 1978).

39   *accurate and faithful* . . . George N. Fenin and William K. Everson, *The Western: From Silents to Cinerama* (New York, Orion Press, 1962).

40   *In the distance, I could see a Western town* . . . Brownlow, *The War, the West, and the Wilderness.*
      Many things happened on that picture . . . Ibid.
      Cinematographer George Schneiderman . . . Ibid.

42   *the momentum of a great nation* . . . Fenin and Everson, *The Western.*

43   *Lincoln is the archetypal figure of justice* . . . McBride, *Searching for John Ford.*
      Tell me, are you the son . . . Carl Sandburg, *Abraham*

Lincoln: The Prairie Years, 1809–1861 (New York: Dell Publishing, 1954).

44 *I'm the big buck of this lick* . . . Ibid.

55 *accepted by the whites* . . . McBride, *Searching for John Ford.*

this vast and constantly-growing agricultural society . . . Smith, *Virgin Land.*

The lack of a fixed address . . . McBride, *Searching for John Ford.*

Time and again, in memoirs and novels . . . Clyde A. Milner II, Carol A. O'Connor, and Martha A. Sandweiss, eds., *The Oxford History of the American West* (New York: Oxford University Press, 1994).

60 *jolting awkwardness in the square dance* . . . McBride, *Searching for John Ford.*

Earp passes between the best values . . . J. A. Place, *The Western Films of John Ford* (Seccaucus, NJ: Citadel Press, 1974).

SIDEBAR: THE REGULARS

65 *as an Irish buffoon* . . . McBride, *Searching for John Ford.*

68 *their hardworking spirit* . . . Ibid.

70 *After half an hour's riding* . . . Parkman, *The Oregon Trail.*

3. THE U.S. CAVALRY AND THE SCARS OF WAR

74 *I had four uncles in the Civil War* . . . Brownlow, *The War, the West, and the Wilderness.*

After the war, the U.S. Army . . . Buscombe, *The BFI Companion to the Western.*

75 *centaurs, superhuman creatures* . . . Fraisse, "Le Far West."

Lindsay Anderson reminds us . . . Lindsay Anderson, *John Ford,* documentary for the BBC series *Omnibus* (1990).

SIDEBAR: JOHN WAYNE

86 *the best picture Ford ever made* . . . Allen Eyles, *John Wayne and the Movies* (South Brunswick, NJ: A. S. Barnes, 1976).

88 *hate John Wayne upholding Goldwater* . . . Ibid.

98 *The cavalry weren't all-American boys* . . . McBride, *Searching for John Ford.*

108 *High up on the top of the tallest bluff* . . . Eyles, *John Wayne.*

110 *the need to bend one's individual will* . . . Place, *The Western Films of John Ford.*

4. FORD AND THE NATIVE AMERICAN

122 *The heart of the Western* . . . Leslie A. Fiedler, *The Return of the Vanishing American* (New York: Stein and Day, 1968).

cleansing him of his hatred . . . Place, *The Western Films of John Ford.*

124 *I believe that the Indian race* . . . Jean-Louis Rieupeyrout, *La grande aventure du Western, 1894–1964* (Paris: Editions du Cerf, 1964).

He noted their lack of "fixed habitation" . . . Parkman, *The Oregon Trail.*

Hunting and fighting . . . Ibid.

130 *Condemned to walk alone* . . . Ralph Friar and Natasha Friar, *The Only Good Indian: The Hollywood Gospel* (New York: Drama Book Specialists, 1972).

In the second decade of the twentieth century . . . Ibid.

From the standpoint of a student . . . *New York Times,* June 3, 1914.

Skinner and other authorities were united . . . Brownlow, *The War, The West, and The Wilderness.*

Rodman Wanamaker's . . . Ibid.

136 *Joseph Breen* . . . McBride, *Searching for John Ford.*

In the paranoid anti-Communist mood . . . Ibid.

138 *lands were being taken up* . . . Smith, *Virgin Land.*

142 *great chests, broad-shouldered* . . . McBride, *Searching for John Ford.*

151 *I've killed more Indians than Custer* . . . Ibid.

trappers [who], to the horror of the genteel hero . . . Smith, *Virgin Land.*

153 *told their people to pack* . . . Dee Brown, *Bury My Heart at Wounded Knee: An Indian History of the American West* (New York: Holt, Rinehart & Winston, 1970).

155 *They made it slow and dreadful* . . . Friar and Friar, *The Only Good Indian.*

156 *Who better than an Irishman* . . . Peter Bogdanovich, *John Ford* (London: MOVIE / Studio Vista, 1967).

5. MONUMENT VALLEY AND FORD'S EXPANSIVE VISION OF THE WEST

161   *a tall, lanky cowboy* . . . Michael F. Blake, *Code of Honor: The Making of Three Great American Westerns* (New York: Taylor Publishing, 2003).
       Malnutrition, disease, unemployment, and alcoholism . . . Dan Ford, *Pappy: The Life of John Ford* (Englewood Cliffs, NJ: Prentice-Hall, 1979).

SIDEBAR: FORD AND THE NAVAJO

162   *It was my happy duty* . . . Cody, *Iron Eyes*.
       shooting arrows into it . . . Ibid.
       John's favorite bit player . . . Ford, *Pappy*.
       Ford spent some sixty thousand dollars . . . McBride, *Searching for John Ford*.

165   *In addition, Ford arranged* . . . Blake, *Code of Honor*.
       [Ford's] been taken into the Navajo tribe . . . Bogdanovich, *John Ford*.
       John Ford runs a close second . . . Blake, *Code of Honor*.

166   *Ford uses [Monument Valley]* . . . Place, *The Western Films of John Ford*.

171   *I tried to copy the Remington style* . . . Bogdanovich, *John Ford*.
       Besides mid-day glare . . . Dippie, *The Frederic Remington Art Museum Collection*.

175   *Ford made Monument Valley* . . . Warner Home Video, *The Turning of the Earth*, documentary for the DVD release of *The Searchers* (2000).

176   *The greatest force in "She Wore a Yellow Ribbon"* . . . Place, *The Western Films of John Ford*.

178   *a nervous wreck* . . . McBride, *Searching for John Ford*.

183   *Commuting through the Irish countryside* . . . Ibid.

185   *John Ford knows* . . . Ibid.

SIDEBAR: MONUMENT VALLEY

186   *I had traveled up there once* . . . Bogdanovich, *John Ford*.
       My favorite location . . . McBride, *Searching for John Ford*.
       We had to lay plank-boards . . . Cody, *Iron Eyes*.

187   *He and the principal actors* . . . Garry Wills, *John Wayne's America: The Politics of Celebrity* (New York: Simon & Schuster, 1997).

189   *the gigantic sculptures* . . . Andrew Sinclair, *John Ford* (New York: Dial Press / James Wade, 1979).

190   *A legend is more interesting* . . . Anderson, documentary.
       the film's visual style . . . Place, *The Western Films of John Ford*.

192   *the almost total* absence *of landscape* . . . McBride, *Searching for John Ford*.
       an unreal stage town . . . Ibid.

193   *an almost slapdash entertainment* . . . *New York Times*, June 3, 1963.

194   *Ford humanizes history* . . . Buscombe, *The BFI Companion to the Western*.

6. THE TELLTALE SIGNATURE

198   *Ford's use of campfire songs* . . . Gilbert Adair, *Flickers: An Illustrated Celebration of 100 Years of Cinema* (London, Boston: Faber and Faber, 1995).
       the extraordinary in the ordinary . . . Rieupeyrout, *La grande aventure du Western*.

199   *It's one of the all-time great shots* . . . Sinclair, *John Ford*.
       Ford's tendency towards bolder visual brush strokes . . . McBride, *Searching for John Ford*.

200   *Sentiment is Jack's vice* . . . Orson Welles and Peter Bogdanovich, *This Is Orson Welles*, ed. Jonathan Rosenbaum (New York: HarperCollins, 1992).

201   *two full pages of analysis* . . . *Libération*, August 27, 2003.

204   *Remington's control of light* . . . Milner, O'Connor, and Sandweiss, *The Oxford History of the American West*.
       Ford, however, looked to Remington . . . McBride, *Searching for John Ford*.
       The gray murk of an approaching storm . . . Bogdanovich, *John Ford*.

205   *I want Remington color* . . . McBride, *Searching for John Ford*.
       such as bathing the sky . . . Blake, *Code of Honor*.

206   *Ford's film "Sergeant Rutledge"* . . . McBride, *Searching for John Ford*.

207   *the greatest vision for a tableau* . . . Ibid.
       Leone "would always talk about Ford" . . . Richard Schickel, *Clint Eastwood: A Biography* (London: Random House, 1996).

211   *the heartbeat of Western myth* . . . Dippie, *The Frederic Remington Art Museum Collection*.

John Ford's Westerns: A Checklist

The Tornado, 1917

The Soul Herder, 1917

Straight Shooting, 1917

A Marked Man, 1917

The Phantom Riders, 1918

Wild Women, 1918

Thieves' Gold, 1918

The Scarlet Drop, 1918

Hell Bent, 1918

Three Mounted Men, 1918

Roped, 1919

The Fighting Brothers, 1919

A Fight for Love, 1919

By Indian Post, 1919

The Rustlers, 1919

Bare Fists, 1919

Gun Law, 1919

The Gun Packer, 1919

Riders of Vengeance, 1919

The Last Outlaw, 1919

The Outcasts of Poker Flat, 1919

The Ace of the Saddle, 1919

The Rider of the Law, 1919

A Gun Fightin' Gentleman, 1919

Marked Men, 1919

Just Pals, 1920

The Freeze Out, 1921

The Wallop, 1921

Desperate Trails, 1921

Action, 1921

Sure Fire, 1921

Three Jumps Ahead, 1923

The Iron Horse, 1924

*3 Bad Men, 1926

Stagecoach, 1939

*Young Mr. Lincoln, 1939

*Drums Along the Mohawk, 1939

My Darling Clementine, 1946

Fort Apache, 1948

*3 Godfathers, 1948

She Wore a Yellow Ribbon, 1949

Wagon Master, 1950

Rio Grande, 1950

The Searchers, 1956

*The Horse Soldiers, 1959

Sergeant Rutledge, 1960

Two Rode Together, 1961

The Man Who Shot Liberty Valance, 1962

*How the West Was Won, Civil War episode, 1962

Cheyenne Autumn, 1964

* films not set in the West but containing
Western elements

Bibliography

American Sublime: Landscape Painting in the United States, 1820–1880. Edited by Andrew Wilton and Tim Barringer. London: Tate Publishing, 2002. An exhibition catalog.

Anderson, Lindsay. *About John Ford.* London: Plexus Publishing, 1999.

Baxter, John. *The Cinema of John Ford.* London: Tantivy Press; New York: A. S. Barnes & Co., 1971.

Blake, Michael F. *Code of Honor: The Making of Three Great American Westerns.* New York: Taylor Publishing, 2003.

Bogdanovich, Peter. *John Ford.* London: MOVIE / Studio Vista, 1967.

Brown, Dee. *Bury My Heart at Wounded Knee: An Indian History of the American West.* New York: Holt, Rinehart & Winston, 1970.

Brownlow, Kevin. *The War, The West, and the Wilderness.* New York: Alfred A. Knopf, 1978.

Buscombe, Ed, ed. *The BFI Companion to the Western.* London: André Deutsch / BFI Publishing, 1988.

———. *Stagecoach.* London: BFI Publishing, 1992.

Cody, Iron Eyes, as told to Collin Perry. *Iron Eyes: My Life as a Hollywood Indian.* New York: Everest House, 1982.

Dippie, Brian W. *The Frederic Remington Art Museum Collection.* New York: Harry N. Abrams, in association with the Frederic Remington Art Museum, 2001.

Eyman, Scott. *Print the Legend: The Life and Times of John Ford.* New York: Simon & Schuster, 1999.

Fenin, George N., and William K. Everson. *The Western: From Silents to Cinerama.* New York: Orion Press, 1962.

Ford, Dan. *Pappy: The Life of John Ford.* Englewood Cliffs, NJ: Prentice-Hall, 1979.

Fraisse, Philippe. "Le Far West: Un imaginaire à la mésure du réel." Special Western issue, *Positif,* nos. 509–10 (July–August 2003).

Friar, Ralph, and Natasha Friar. *The Only Good Indian: The Hollywood Gospel.* New York: Drama Book Specialists, 1972.

Gabarscek, Carlo. *Il West di John Ford.* Friuli, Italy: Arti Grafiche Friulane, 1994.

Gallagher, Tag. *John Ford: The Man and His Films.* Berkeley: University of California Press, 1986.

McBride, Joseph. *Searching for John Ford: A Life.* New York: St. Martin's Press, 2001.

McBride, Joseph, and Michael Wilmington. *John Ford.* London: Secker and Warburg, 1974.

Milner, Clyde A., II, Carol A. O'Connor, and Martha A. Sandweiss, eds. *The Oxford History of the American West.* New York: Oxford University Press, 1994.

Parkman, Francis. *The Oregon Trail.* New York: George P. Putnam, 1849.

Place, J. A. *The Western Films of John Ford.* Secaucus, NJ: Citadel Press, 1974.

Rieupeyrout, Jean-Louis. *La grande aventure du Western, 1894–1964.* Paris: Editions du Cerf, 1964.

Sarris, Andrew. *The John Ford Movie Mystery.* London: Secker and Warburg, 1976.

Sinclair, Andrew. *John Ford.* New York: Dial Press / James Wade, 1979.

Smith, Henry Nash. *Virgin Land: The American West as Symbol and Myth.* Cambridge, MA: Harvard University Press, 1950.

Spittles, Brian. *John Ford.* Harlow, UK: Longman (Pearson Education), 2002.

Turner, Frederick Jackson. *The Frontier in American History.* New York: Dover Publications, 1996.

Zimmerman, Larry J., and Brian Leigh Molyneaux, eds. *Native North America.* Boston: Little Brown & Co., 1997.

Acknowledgments

I am particularly grateful to Eric Himmel, editor-in-chief at Harry N. Abrams, Inc., who believed in this book from the outset. My editors at Abrams, Harriet Whelchel and Richard Slovak, have proved both efficient and perceptive, helping to shape the book into a coherent whole. I am grateful to Miko McGinty for her imaginative graphic design for this book. My thanks go also to David Lee Clark (who guided me through Monument Valley), Lorenzo Codelli, Michael Dorr, Alan Rutsky, and John Webber, as well as my agent, Laura Morris, and my ever-patient wife, Françoise.

For photographs, I am indebted first and foremost to Dave Kent and the Kobal Collection, and also to André Chevailler and his team at the stills library of La Cinémathèque Suisse. The various museums and sources of illustrations are listed separately, but I would like to acknowledge the pioneering work of Carlo Gabarscek, several of whose photographs of Monument Valley I include here, and whose knowledge of the locations used for Hollywood Westerns is unparalleled.

Credits

Index

Page numbers in *italics* refer to captions for illustrations.

Monument Valley's "John Ford Point" appears in various Ford Westerns.